PROFESSOR HILL PRESENTS

SANGAKU™ #2

The World's Greatest Number Puzzles!

James D. Hill

Skyhorse Publishing

Skyhorse Publishing books may be purchased in bulk at special discounts for sales promotion, corporate gifts, fund-raising, or educational purposes. Special editions can also be created to specifications. For details, contact the Special Sales Department, Skyhorse Publishing, 307 West 36th Street, 11th Floor, New York, NY 10018 or info@skyhorsepublishing.com.

Skyhorse® and Skyhorse Publishing® are registered trademarks of Skyhorse Publishing, Inc.®, a Delaware corporation.

Visit our website at www.skyhorsepublishing.com.

10 9 8 7 6 5 4 3 2 1

Library of Congress Cataloging-in-Publication Data is available on file.

ISBN: 978-1-62636-423-3

Printed in China

SANGAKU™ #2

Table of Contents

— *More Than 200 Puzzles!* —

INTRODUCTION

In 2200 B.C. the legendary Emperor Yu was the ruler of China. Being an emperor in those days was very stressful. Among his many worries and responsibilities were protecting the Empire from invasion, building a strong military, and contending with the floods of the Yellow River. To help relieve this tension, he often took a stroll along the banks of the Yellow River. One day as he walked along the river bank he saw a tortoise emerge from the river. It slowly crawled, seemingly unafraid, right up to Emperor Yu's feet. There on the back of the tortoise was a strange decoration (see Fig. 1). The decoration became known as "Lo-Shu." It consisted of nine numbers arranged in a 3x3 grid. The numbers were represented by dots connected with lines: black dots for the even numbers and white dots for the odd numbers. These numbers were arranged so that if one added together any three numbers in a line, even diagonally, the result was a sum of 15.

Emperor Yu was so impressed by this event that he interpreted it as a message from God. He thought it must be divine, considering its mystic harmony and curious symmetry! Was it a good omen or a bad omen? Did it mean a long life or impending death? Emperor Yu had just observed the *world's first number puzzle*. However, this was not the first recording of the Lo-Shu. The Lo-Shu goes back another six hundred years to 2800 B.C. when Fuh-Hi is credited with its recording in his scroll, "The Scroll of the River Lo." Today the Lo-Shu is known as the 3x3 "magic square" (see Fig. 2).

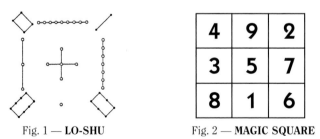

Fig. 1 — **LO-SHU**   Fig. 2 — **MAGIC SQUARE**

Down through the centuries the magic square has been found in India, Africa, and almost every continent on Earth. It was found in the ruins of the Mayan civilization of Mexico, in Central America, and scratched on the walls of ancient caves in Northern France.

Many others have marveled at the mathematical characteristics of the magic square. Benjamin Franklin was a disciple of the magic square, along with artists, mathematicians, scientists, philosophers, and others. Some were so overcome by its mystical properties that they believed it held secrets of the universe. Gerber, an Islamic alchemist, was sure that the magic square could reveal a hidden formula by which metal could be turned to gold. The magic square was used as a talisman to ward off evil spirits and to ease the pain of childbirth. It was displayed on a home's exterior for protection and worn into battle to assure victory.

Is it what we make numbers do, or what numbers make us do? Numbers are just numbers, aren't they? Or are they?

When I first became aware of magic squares over thirty years ago, I too was fascinated with their unusual mathematical properties. I discovered that there were magic squares other than the Lo-Shu 3x3 (order 3); there were 4x4 (order 4, where sixteen numbers were used), 5x5 (order 5, where twenty-five numbers were used) and on and on and on. For the average person, working with so many numbers quickly becomes frustrating.

I searched diligently for "number sum puzzles" other than the magic squares and found only a few. It was then that I decided to create Professor Hill's™ number puzzles. My goal was to create puzzles that would entertain all age groups and encompass all levels of difficulty from easy, to moderate, to difficult, to very difficult. Not wanting to restrict my puzzles to squares, I used many geometric configurations. Professor Hill's™ number puzzles are original, classic, and unique with care and thought put into each and every one to make them as exciting and challenging as possible for the targeted difficulty level and age group. There is a strong demand for number puzzles which challenge the mental processes. Professor Hill's™ number puzzles will satisfy that demand!

Why "**SANGAKU**™"? During the Edo period (1603–1867), Japan isolated itself from the western world. Although some would view this isolation and lack of interaction as a form of "dark age," in actuality, it fostered a form of Japanese mathematical self-discovery and renaissance. It was during this isolation that the Japanese people produced mathematical theorems, including advanced concepts in Euclidean geometry. In some cases these theorems predated their discovery in the western world. These mathematical theorems were presented as vibrantly colored drawings on wooden tablets which were hung in Shinto shrines and temples. These were called "Sangaku," votive tablets featuring mathematical puzzles. Because the solution was often not provided, the Sangaku hanging in the shrine or temple represented not only an offering to the shrine, but a mathematical challenge that its viewers must contemplate and solve.

It is in Sangaku's spirit of mathematical challenge and contemplation that I have designed my puzzles, and due to that same spirit of challenge, I have chosen to call them **SANGAKU**™.

— James D. Hill

THE UNIVERSE, SYMMETRY, AND THE NUMERATE ZONE

The symmetry, magic, and mystery of numbers reach into the core of our material universe and into the heart and soul of our human understanding. Aristotle said, "The chief forms of beauty are order and symmetry, which the mathematical sciences demonstrate in a special degree." Nature is filled with symmetry and mystery—from the unique and random regularity found in each snowflake, to the pairs of opposites found in atoms (i.e. protons and electrons), to the existence of both matter and antimatter, dark energy and dark matter, order and chaos, superstrings and ten dimensions, and the seeming contradiction between the totally predictable clockwork universe described by Newton and the completely unpredictable subatomic world described by quantum physics and its uncertainty principle. And the keys to unlocking the secrets of nature are the language of mathematics and its alphabet soup of numbers and symbols. Numbers are the magic code which gives us the wizardry to explore the hidden secrets found deep within the mysteries of matter, energy, space, and time.

It should not be surprising, therefore, that numbers themselves encompass symmetry and patterns of near mystical design. Poets tell us that time is the tide of man's fortunes, a flowing river which carries us from conception to death—a child of human hopes, dreams, nightmares, and fears. But Einstein tells us that time is invention and illusion, a gossamer web which is stretched and shaped by velocity and gravity, and that it is only one of the multitude of variables which make up our universe as defined by $E=MC^2$, his greatest equation. Indeed, under relativity, time is barely more than a ghost in the fabric of space, and only the second or lesser half of the space-time continuum. Without matter, change, or motion, that is, before the Big Bang, when the universe was still merely an equation in the mind of God, time did not exist at all.

From our earliest philosophers to our most modern physicists, it has been recognized that there is a vital link between the magic of numbers and the cosmos around us of which we are a part. Professor Hill's puzzles inexorably draw us into the realm of that magic. In working and solving these puzzles, we not only see the symmetry and order which are revealed by their solution, but we actually feel and experience the mystery and wonder which the numbers encode. In delving deeply into the **NUMERATE ZONE**, you may truly reach an entrancing and mystical state. At the very least you will have a whale of a good time. But enter with care. Like a quest for the infinite and the divine, a journey into the **NUMERATE ZONE** can be very seductive, intoxicating, and even addictive. Nevertheless, you will truly love the fun and joy of this marvelous adventure.

— Ben Johnson Talbott, Jr.

(Editor's Note: Talbott is a graduate of Harvard Law School and Xavier University, magna cum laude. He was a Presidential appointee to the Board of Directors of America's Defense Enterprise Fund, and he is listed in Who's Who in American Law, Who's Who in America, *and* Who's Who in the World.*)*

WARNING!!!

Professor Hill's™ Number Puzzles are addictive! The solver will be captivated and mesmerized by the harmonious arrangement and alluring symmetry of numbers. The solver will be drawn into a new dimension of number puzzles: the ***Numerate Zone***. The ***Numerate Zone*** is an adventurous journey into a world of numbers never before explored. The ***Numerate Zone*** has a magnetic attraction equaled only by the vortex well of a black hole. After entering this zone, one may not go back. When in the ***Numerate Zone*** a void is created that cannot be filled, a habitual craving that cannot be satisfied, except with more Professor Hill's™ Number Puzzles. The solvers' quests will be justly rewarded.

You are now entering the

Numerate Zone!

SOLVING SANGAKU™ "SAME SUM" NUMBER PUZZLES

Same Sum Number Puzzles are geometric figures consisting of circles connected by lines. The figures take on many shapes. These puzzles are solved by arranging a given set of numbers in the circles of the geometric figure so that lines and groups of numbers have the same sum (see the sample puzzle below).

Next to the puzzle are the set of numbers to be used (1-8), the sum (13) and four miniature puzzles showing the highlighted groups of circles with the given sums.

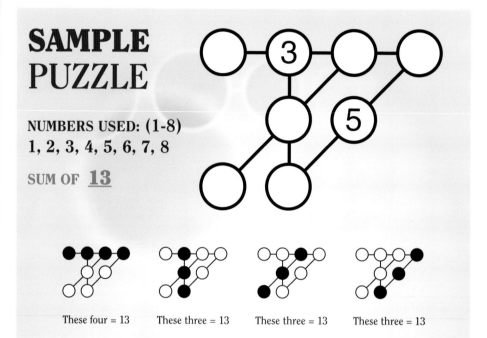

SAMPLE PUZZLE

NUMBERS USED: (1-8)
1, 2, 3, 4, 5, 6, 7, 8

SUM OF **13**

These four = 13   These three = 13   These three = 13   These three = 13

In this puzzle there are four groups of numbers that must have the same sum of 13 — one group of four numbers and three groups of three numbers.

ANSWER

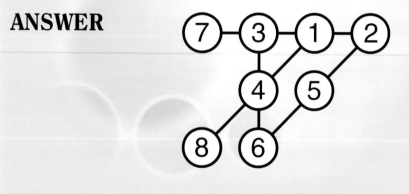

NOTE: ALMOST ALL PUZZLES HAVE MORE THAN ONE SOLUTION.

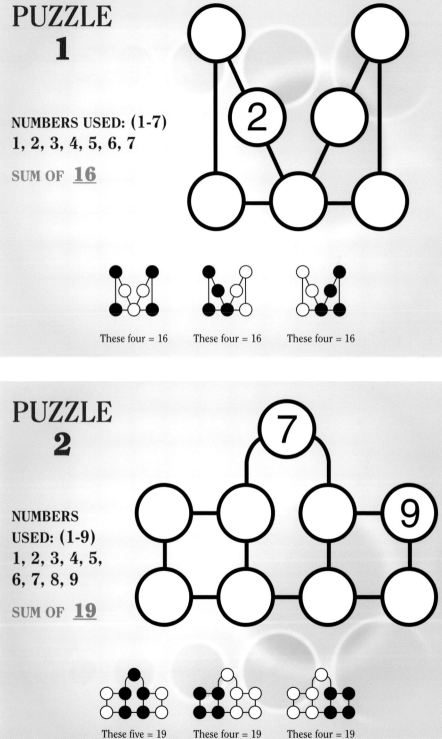

PUZZLE 1

NUMBERS USED: (1-7)
1, 2, 3, 4, 5, 6, 7

SUM OF **16**

These four = 16   These four = 16   These four = 16

PUZZLE 2

NUMBERS USED: (1-9)
1, 2, 3, 4, 5, 6, 7, 8, 9

SUM OF **19**

These five = 19   These four = 19   These four = 19

PUZZLE 3

NUMBERS USED: (1-8)
1, 2, 3, 4, 5, 6, 7, 8

SUM OF __14__

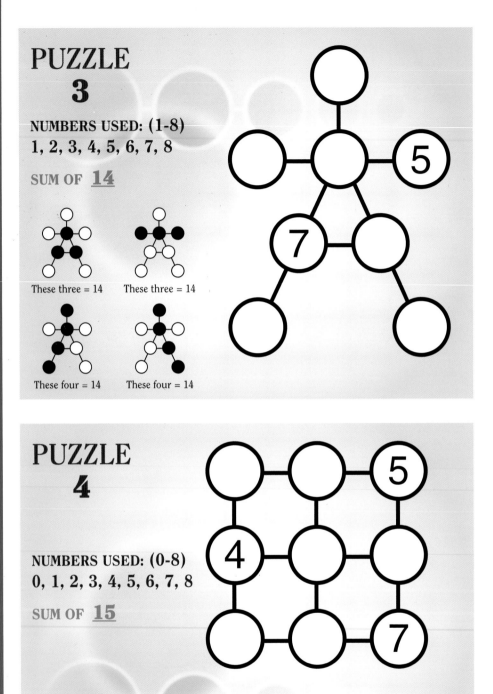

These three = 14   These three = 14

These four = 14   These four = 14

PUZZLE 4

NUMBERS USED: (0-8)
0, 1, 2, 3, 4, 5, 6, 7, 8

SUM OF __15__

These four = 15   These four = 15   These four = 15   These four = 15

DIRECTIONS FOR SOLVING ARE ON PAGE 8   ANSWERS ON PAGE 118

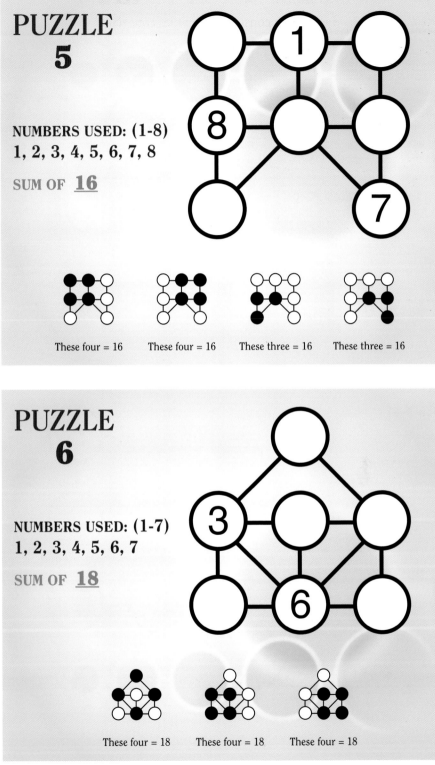

PUZZLE 5

NUMBERS USED: (1-8)
1, 2, 3, 4, 5, 6, 7, 8

SUM OF 16

These four = 16   These four = 16   These three = 16   These three = 16

PUZZLE 6

NUMBERS USED: (1-7)
1, 2, 3, 4, 5, 6, 7

SUM OF 18

These four = 18   These four = 18   These four = 18

DIRECTIONS FOR SOLVING ARE ON PAGE 8   ANSWERS ON PAGE 118

PUZZLE 7

NUMBERS USED: (0-9)
0, 1, 2, 3, 4,
5, 6, 7, 8, 9

SUM OF **15**

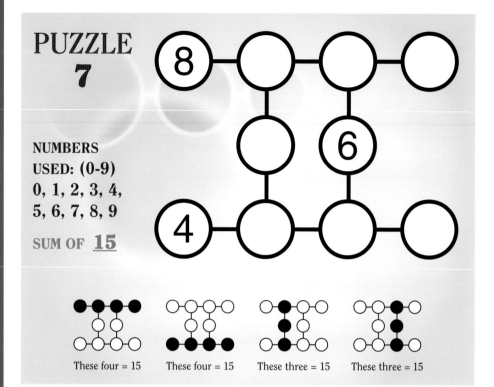

These four = 15   These four = 15   These three = 15   These three = 15

PUZZLE 8

NUMBERS USED: (1-7)
1, 2, 3, 4, 5, 6, 7

SUM OF **14**

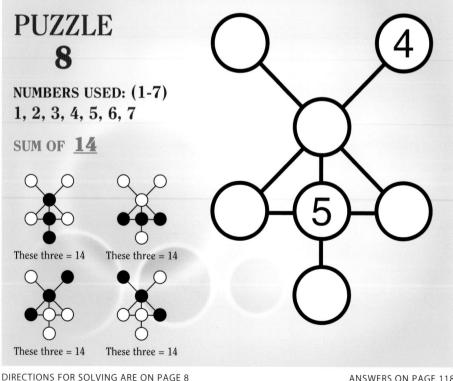

These three = 14   These three = 14

These three = 14   These three = 14

DIRECTIONS FOR SOLVING ARE ON PAGE 8   ANSWERS ON PAGE 118

PUZZLE 9

NUMBERS USED:
1, 1, 2, 2, 3, 3, 4, 4

SUM OF 11

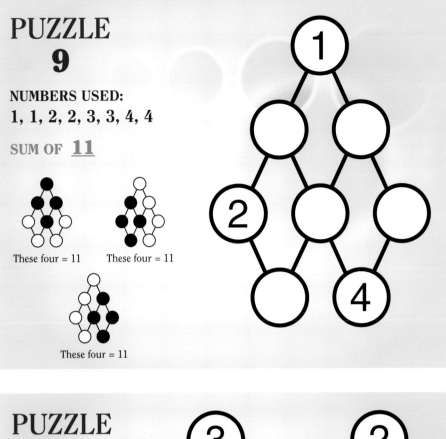

These four = 11   These four = 11

These four = 11

PUZZLE 10

NUMBERS USED: (1-7)
1, 2, 3, 4, 5, 6, 7

SUM OF 17

These three = 17   These four = 17   These four = 17

DIRECTIONS FOR SOLVING ARE ON PAGE 8   ANSWERS ON PAGE 118

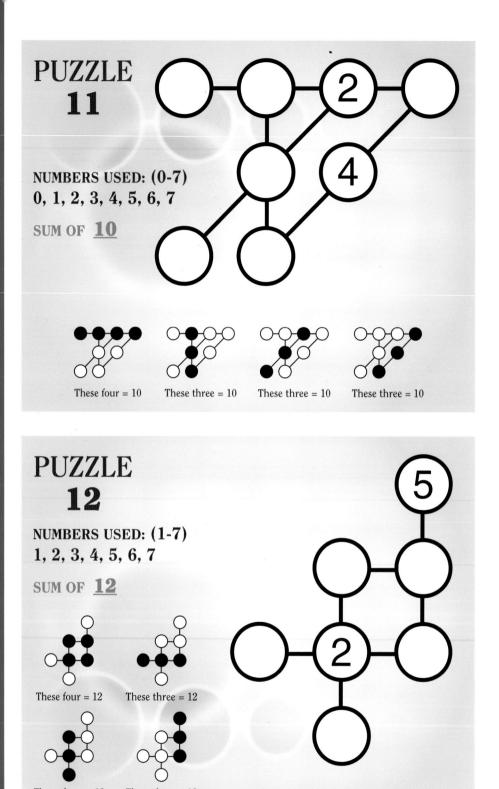

PUZZLE 11

NUMBERS USED: (0-7)
0, 1, 2, 3, 4, 5, 6, 7

SUM OF **10**

These four = 10   These three = 10   These three = 10   These three = 10

PUZZLE 12

NUMBERS USED: (1-7)
1, 2, 3, 4, 5, 6, 7

SUM OF **12**

These four = 12   These three = 12

These three = 12   These three = 12

PUZZLE 13

NUMBERS USED: (1-9)
1, 2, 3, 4, 5, 6, 7, 8, 9

SUM OF 20

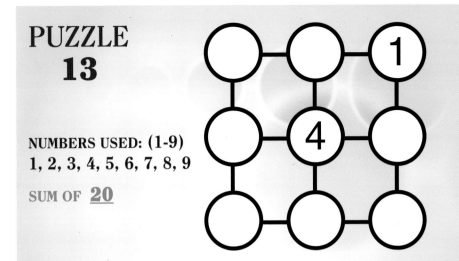

 These four = 20   These four = 20   These four = 20   These four = 20

PUZZLE 14

NUMBERS USED: (1-9)
1, 2, 3, 4, 5, 6, 7, 8, 9

SUM OF 20

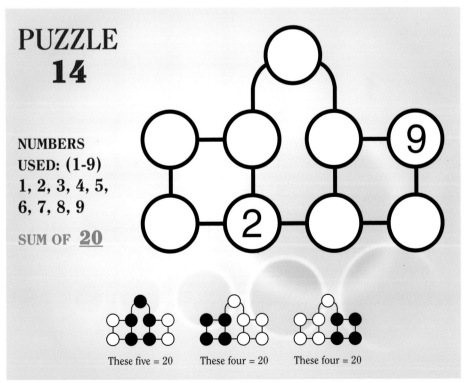

These five = 20   These four = 20   These four = 20

DIRECTIONS FOR SOLVING ARE ON PAGE 8

ANSWERS ON PAGE 118

PUZZLE 15

NUMBERS USED: (1-8)
1, 2, 3, 4, 5, 6, 7, 8

SUM OF **15**

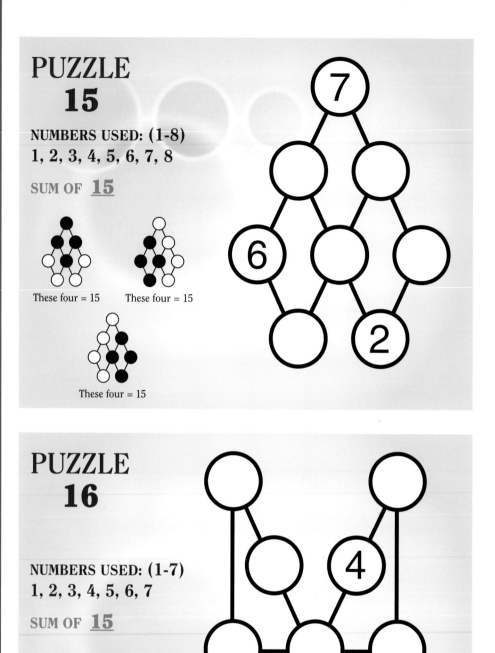

These four = 15

These four = 15

These four = 15

PUZZLE 16

NUMBERS USED: (1-7)
1, 2, 3, 4, 5, 6, 7

SUM OF **15**

These three = 15

These four = 15

These four = 15

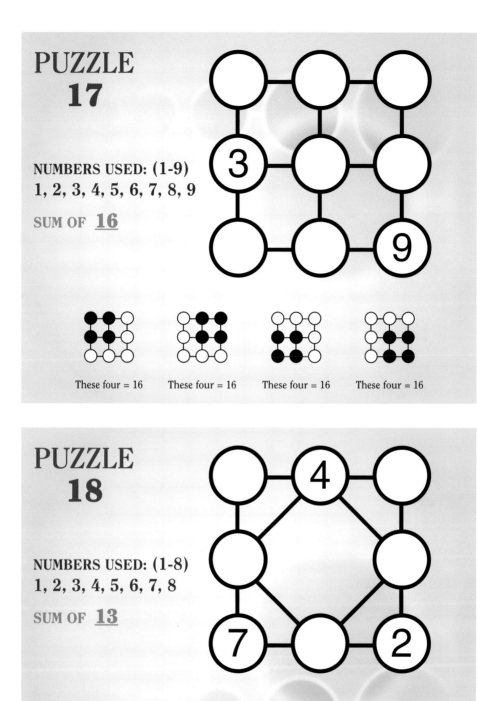

PUZZLE 17

NUMBERS USED: (1-9)
1, 2, 3, 4, 5, 6, 7, 8, 9

SUM OF **16**

These four = 16   These four = 16   These four = 16   These four = 16

PUZZLE 18

NUMBERS USED: (1-8)
1, 2, 3, 4, 5, 6, 7, 8

SUM OF **13**

These three = 13   These three = 13   These three = 13   These three = 13

DIRECTIONS FOR SOLVING ARE ON PAGE 8   ANSWERS ON PAGE 119

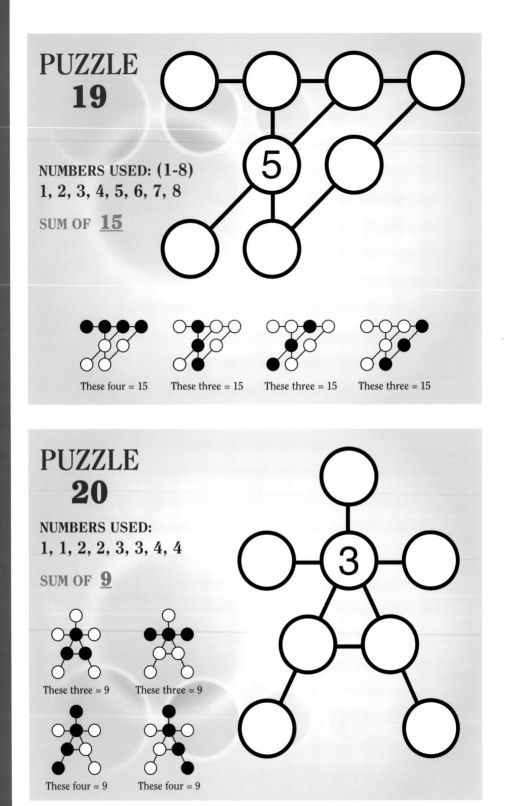

PUZZLE 19

NUMBERS USED: (1-8)
1, 2, 3, 4, 5, 6, 7, 8

SUM OF **15**

These four = 15   These three = 15   These three = 15   These three = 15

PUZZLE 20

NUMBERS USED:
1, 1, 2, 2, 3, 3, 4, 4

SUM OF **9**

These three = 9   These three = 9

These four = 9   These four = 9

DIRECTIONS FOR SOLVING ARE ON PAGE 8   ANSWERS ON PAGE 119

PUZZLE 21

NUMBERS USED: (1-8)
1, 2, 3, 4, 5, 6, 7, 8

SUM OF **13**

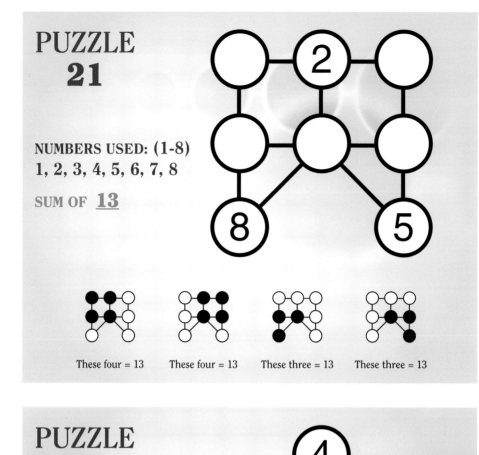

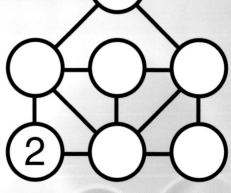

| These four = 13 | These four = 13 | These three = 13 | These three = 13 |

PUZZLE 22

NUMBERS USED: (0-6)
0, 1, 2, 3, 4, 5, 6

SUM OF **10**

These four = 10   These four = 10   These four = 10

SOLVING SANGAKU™ "HONEYCOMB" NUMBER PUZZLES

Honeycomb Number Puzzle designs consist of connecting hexagons (six-sided figures). There may be any number of hexagons in a puzzle design. Numbers are located along the perimeter of each design (see below). These numbers represent the sum of all the numbers in that particular line or row of hexagons. Arrowheads are placed around the perimeter to direct the solver in calculating a particular line or row of hexagons. To solve a Honeycomb Puzzle, arrange a given set of numbers correctly to arrive at the given sums. Do not place numbers in the shaded spaces. Below are two sample puzzles with the answers.

#1 SAMPLE

USE THE NUMBERS: (1-8)
1, 2, 3, 4, 5, 6, 7, 8

SAMPLE 1 ANSWER

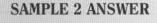
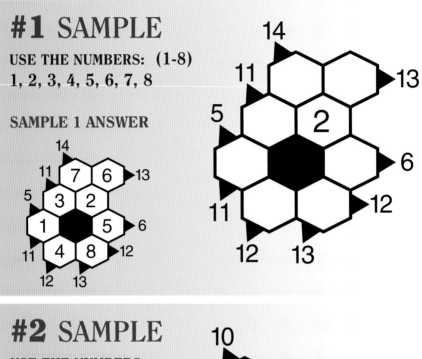

#2 SAMPLE

USE THE NUMBERS:
1, 1, 2, 2, 3, 3, 4, 4

SAMPLE 2 ANSWER

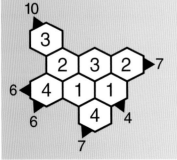
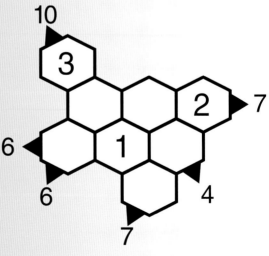

NOTE: ALMOST ALL PUZZLES HAVE MORE THAN ONE SOLUTION.

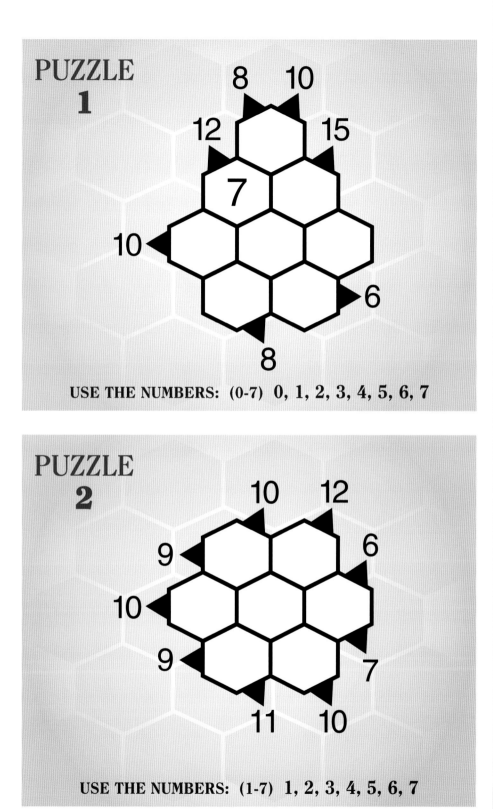

PUZZLE **1**

USE THE NUMBERS: (0-7) **0, 1, 2, 3, 4, 5, 6, 7**

PUZZLE **2**

USE THE NUMBERS: (1-7) **1, 2, 3, 4, 5, 6, 7**

DIRECTIONS FOR SOLVING ARE ON PAGE 20   ANSWERS ON PAGE 119

PUZZLE 3

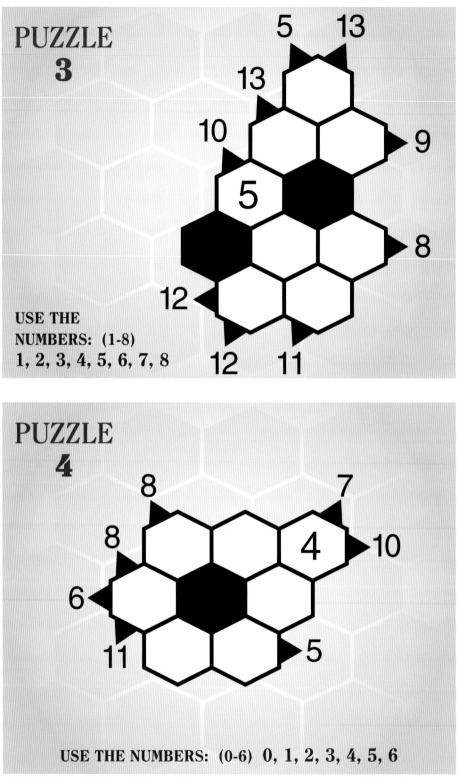

USE THE
NUMBERS: (1-8)
1, 2, 3, 4, 5, 6, 7, 8

PUZZLE 4

USE THE NUMBERS: (0-6) 0, 1, 2, 3, 4, 5, 6

DIRECTIONS FOR SOLVING ARE ON PAGE 20   ANSWERS ON PAGE 119

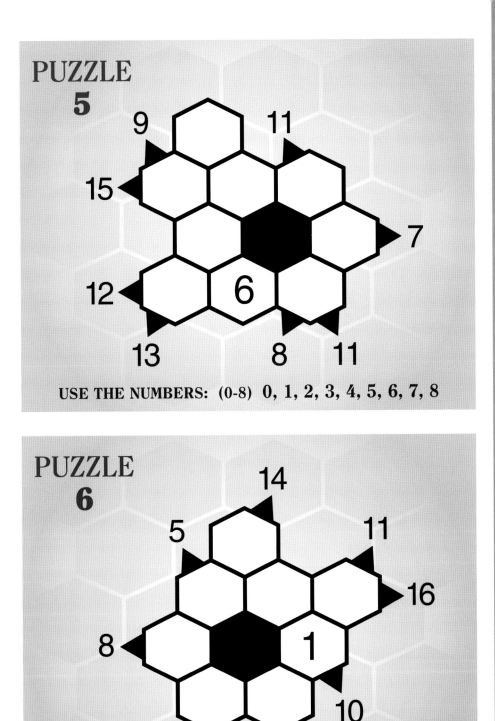

PUZZLE 5

9 11

15

7

12

6

13 8 11

USE THE NUMBERS: (0-8) 0, 1, 2, 3, 4, 5, 6, 7, 8

PUZZLE 6

14

5 11

16

8

1

10

USE THE NUMBERS: (1-8) 1, 2, 3, 4, 5, 6, 7, 8

DIRECTIONS FOR SOLVING ARE ON PAGE 20 ANSWERS ON PAGE 119

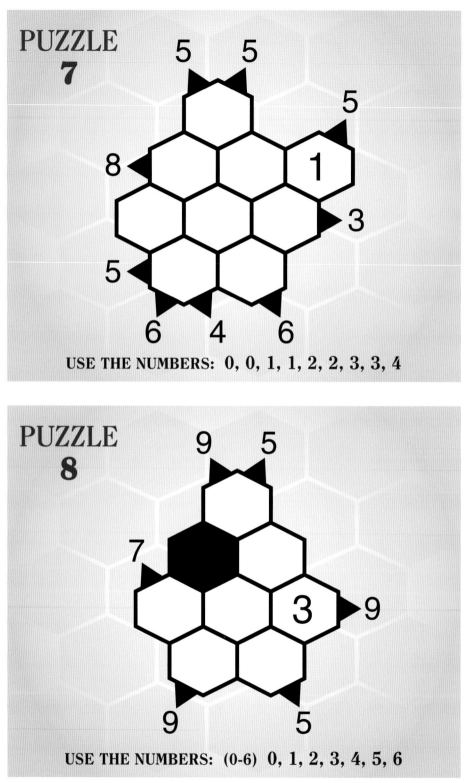

PUZZLE 7

5 5

5

8

1

3

5

6 4 6

USE THE NUMBERS: 0, 0, 1, 1, 2, 2, 3, 3, 4

PUZZLE 8

9 5

7

3 9

9 5

USE THE NUMBERS: (0-6) 0, 1, 2, 3, 4, 5, 6

DIRECTIONS FOR SOLVING ARE ON PAGE 20   ANSWERS ON PAGE 119

PUZZLE 9

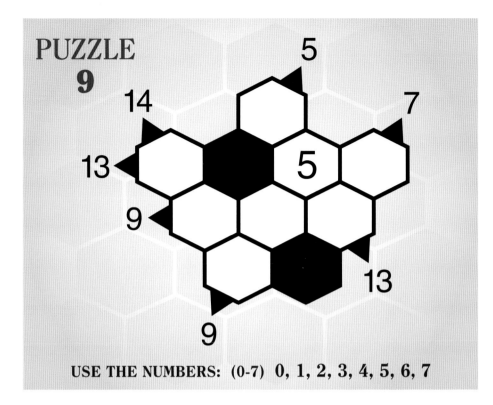

USE THE NUMBERS: (0-7) 0, 1, 2, 3, 4, 5, 6, 7

PUZZLE 10

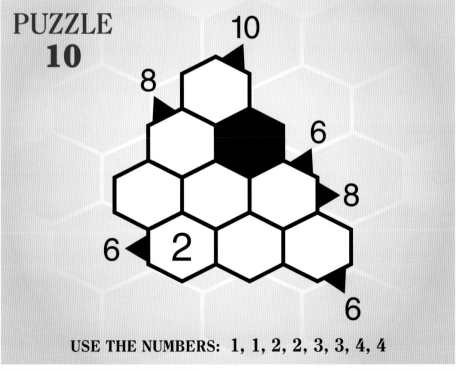

USE THE NUMBERS: 1, 1, 2, 2, 3, 3, 4, 4

DIRECTIONS FOR SOLVING ARE ON PAGE 20   ANSWERS ON PAGE 120

PUZZLE 11

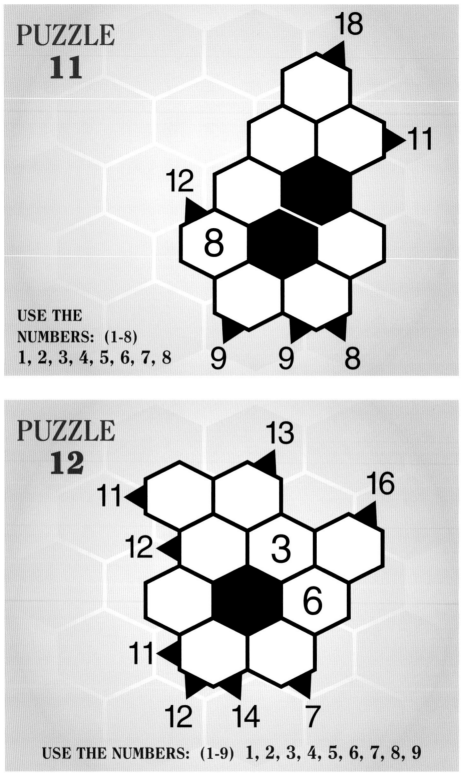

USE THE NUMBERS: (1-8)
1, 2, 3, 4, 5, 6, 7, 8

18

11

12

8

9   9   8

PUZZLE 12

13

16

11

12

3

6

11

12   14   7

USE THE NUMBERS: (1-9) 1, 2, 3, 4, 5, 6, 7, 8, 9

PUZZLE 13

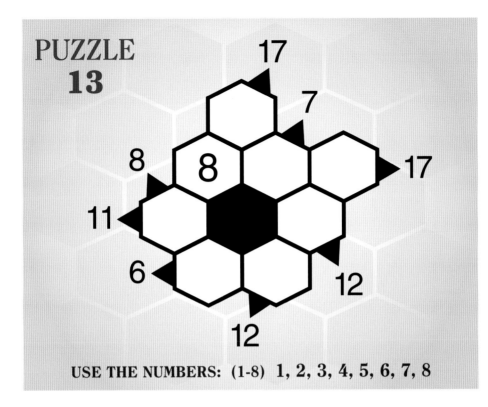

USE THE NUMBERS: (1-8) 1, 2, 3, 4, 5, 6, 7, 8

PUZZLE 14

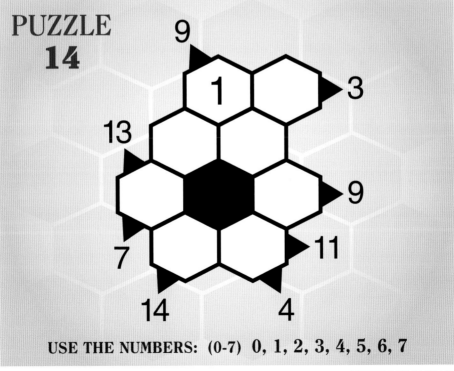

USE THE NUMBERS: (0-7) 0, 1, 2, 3, 4, 5, 6, 7

DIRECTIONS FOR SOLVING ARE ON PAGE 20   ANSWERS ON PAGE 120

PUZZLE 15

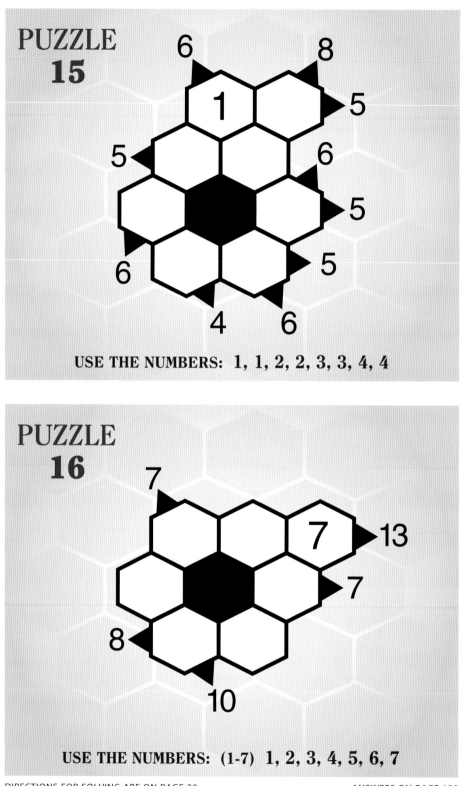

USE THE NUMBERS: 1, 1, 2, 2, 3, 3, 4, 4

PUZZLE 16

USE THE NUMBERS: (1-7) 1, 2, 3, 4, 5, 6, 7

DIRECTIONS FOR SOLVING ARE ON PAGE 20   ANSWERS ON PAGE 120

PUZZLE 17

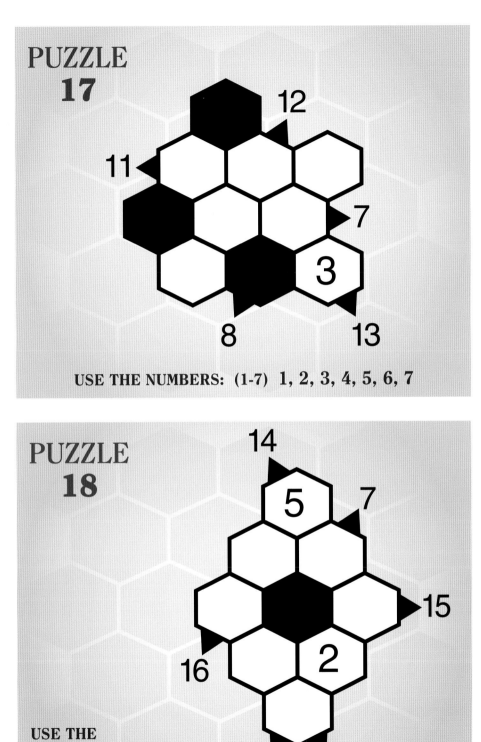

12

11

7

3

8   13

USE THE NUMBERS: (1-7) 1, 2, 3, 4, 5, 6, 7

PUZZLE 18

14

5   7

15

16

2

16

13   16

**USE THE NUMBERS: (1-8)
1, 2, 3, 4, 5, 6, 7, 8**

DIRECTIONS FOR SOLVING ARE ON PAGE 20   ANSWERS ON PAGE 120

PUZZLE 19

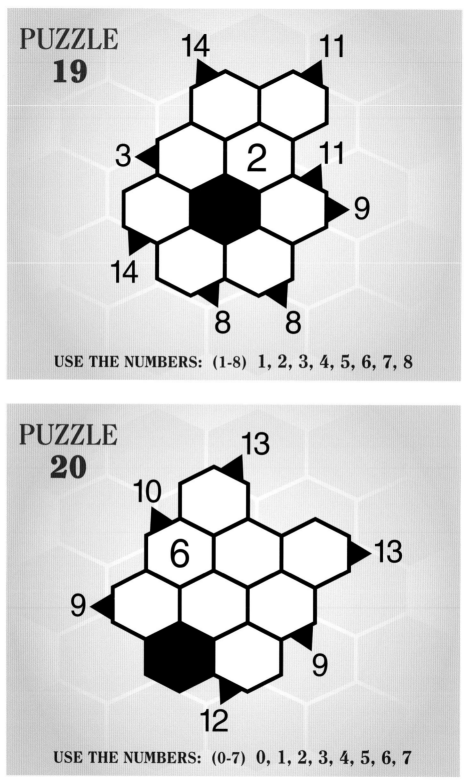

14   11

3   2   11

9

14

8   8

USE THE NUMBERS: (1-8) 1, 2, 3, 4, 5, 6, 7, 8

PUZZLE 20

13

10

6

9   13

9

12

USE THE NUMBERS: (0-7) 0, 1, 2, 3, 4, 5, 6, 7

DIRECTIONS FOR SOLVING ARE ON PAGE 20   ANSWERS ON PAGE 120

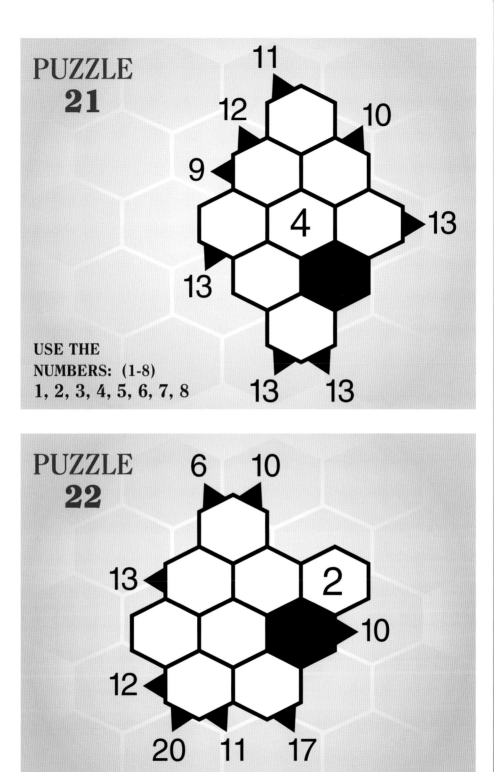

PUZZLE 21

11

12   10

9

4

13

13

13

USE THE
NUMBERS: (1-8)
1, 2, 3, 4, 5, 6, 7, 8

13   13

PUZZLE 22

6   10

13   2

10

12

20   11   17

USE THE NUMBERS: (1-8) 1, 2, 3, 4, 5, 6, 7, 8

DIRECTIONS FOR SOLVING ARE ON PAGE 20   ANSWERS ON PAGE 120

PUZZLE 23

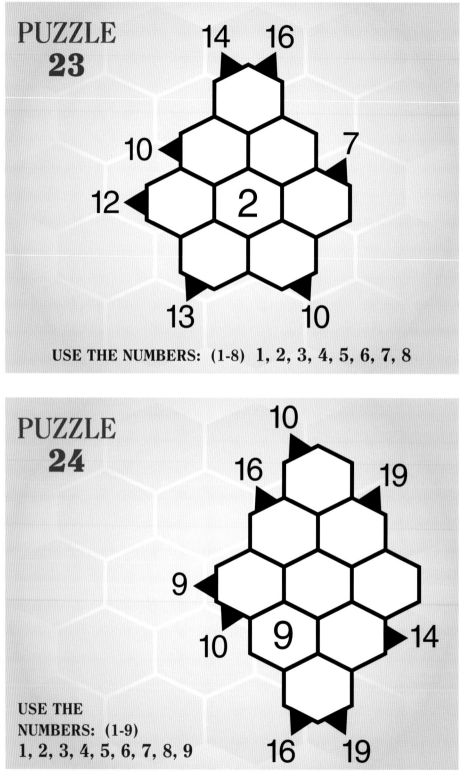

14   16

10   7

12   2

13   10

USE THE NUMBERS: (1-8) 1, 2, 3, 4, 5, 6, 7, 8

PUZZLE 24

10

16   19

9

10   9   14

USE THE NUMBERS: (1-9) 1, 2, 3, 4, 5, 6, 7, 8, 9

16   19

DIRECTIONS FOR SOLVING ARE ON PAGE 20   ANSWERS ON PAGE 120

SOLVING SANGAKU™ "CHOPSTICK" NUMBER PUZZLES

Chopstick Number Puzzles consist of straight lines (3-6) that resemble chopsticks. Circles are placed randomly on the chopsticks. At the end of each chopstick are numbers, which represent the sums of all the numbers to be placed in that particular chopstick. To solve each puzzle, place a given set of numbers in the circles to arrive at the sums shown.

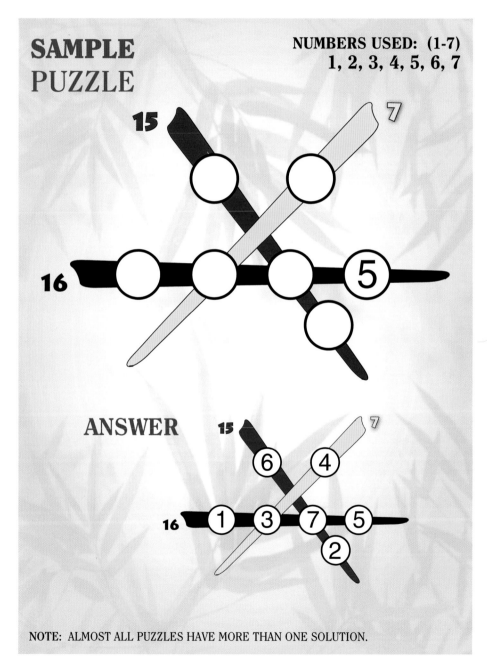

SAMPLE PUZZLE

NUMBERS USED: (1-7)
1, 2, 3, 4, 5, 6, 7

ANSWER

NOTE: ALMOST ALL PUZZLES HAVE MORE THAN ONE SOLUTION.

PUZZLE 1

NUMBERS USED: (0-6)
0, 1, 2, 3, 4, 5, 6

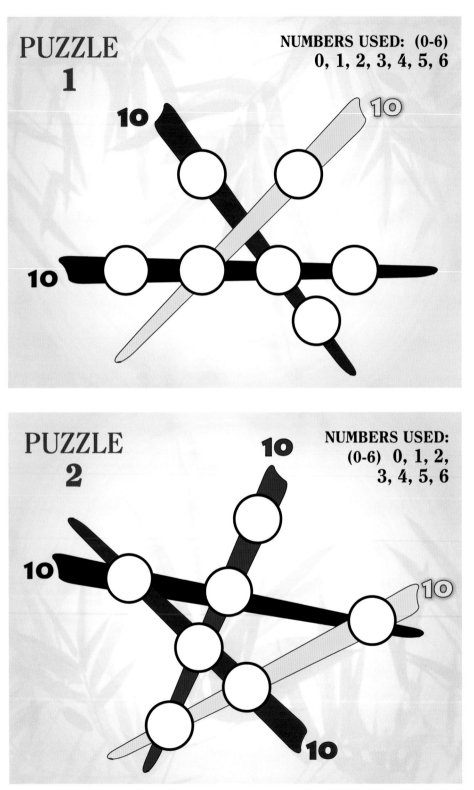

PUZZLE 2

NUMBERS USED:
(0-6) 0, 1, 2,
3, 4, 5, 6

DIRECTIONS FOR SOLVING ARE ON PAGE 33   ANSWERS ON PAGE 121

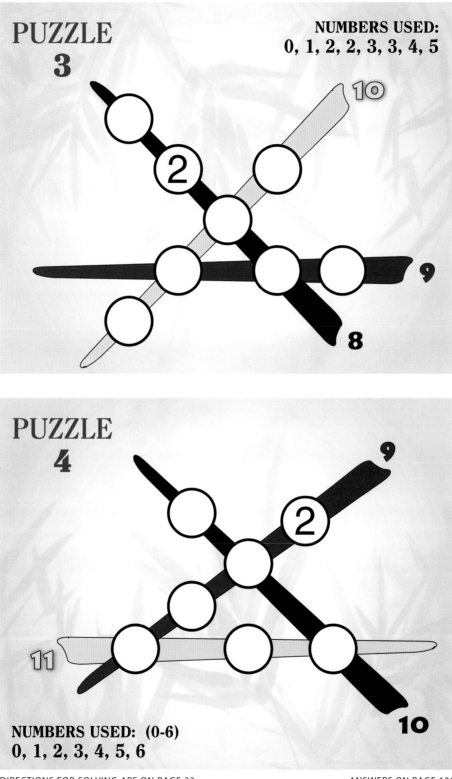

PUZZLE
3

NUMBERS USED:
0, 1, 2, 2, 3, 3, 4, 5

10

2

9

8

PUZZLE
4

9

2

11

NUMBERS USED: (0-6)
0, 1, 2, 3, 4, 5, 6

10

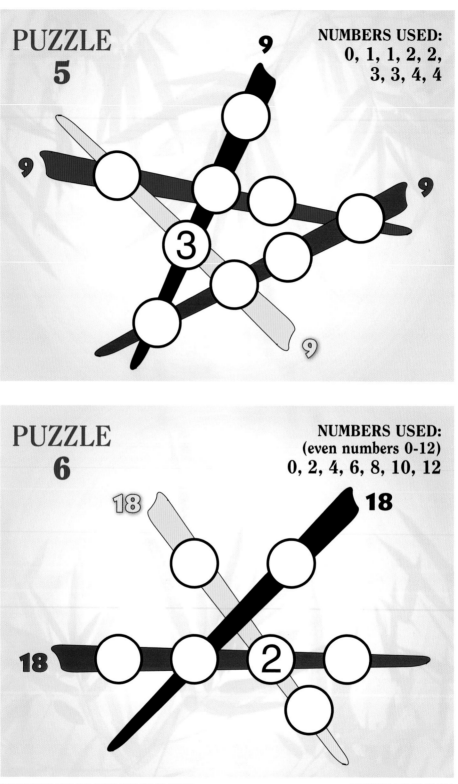

PUZZLE 5

9

9

9

3

9

PUZZLE 6

18

18

18

2

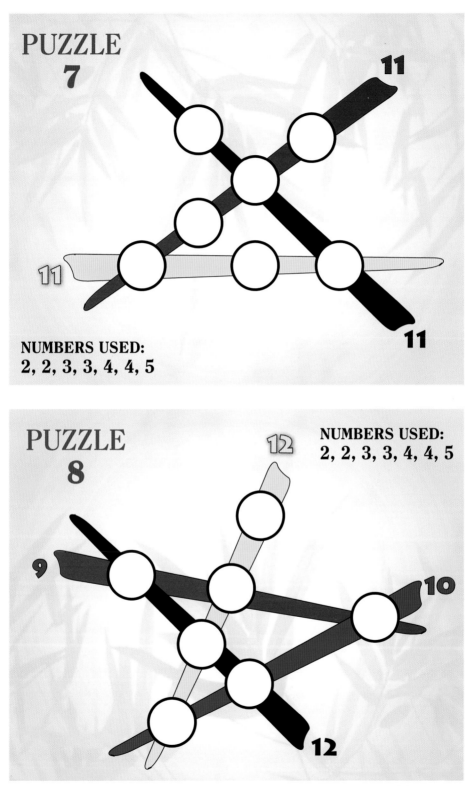

PUZZLE 7

11

11

11

NUMBERS USED:
2, 2, 3, 3, 4, 4, 5

PUZZLE 8

12

NUMBERS USED:
2, 2, 3, 3, 4, 4, 5

9

10

12

DIRECTIONS FOR SOLVING ARE ON PAGE 33

ANSWERS ON PAGE 121

PUZZLE 9

NUMBERS USED: (1-7)
1, 2, 3, 4, 5, 6, 7

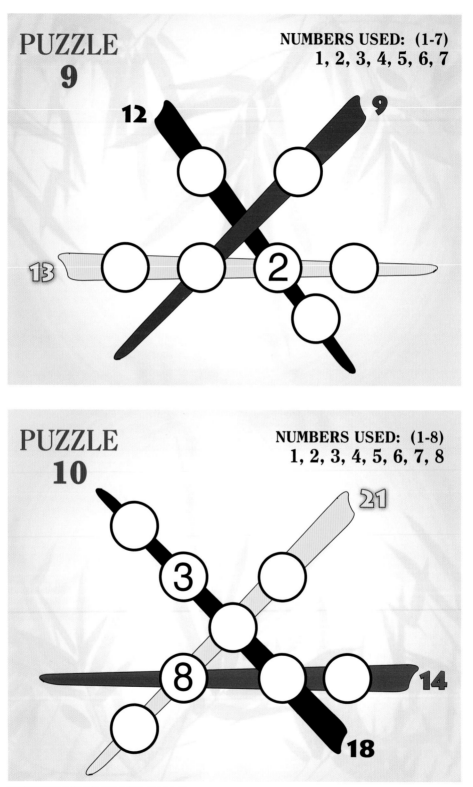

12

9

13

2

PUZZLE 10

NUMBERS USED: (1-8)
1, 2, 3, 4, 5, 6, 7, 8

21

3

8

14

18

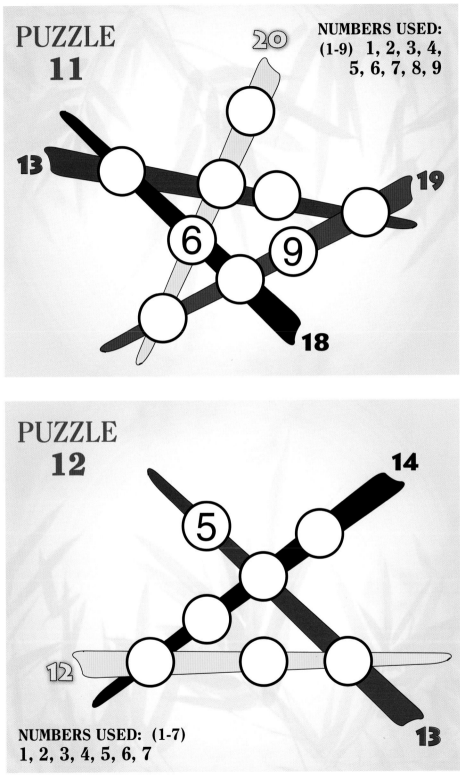

PUZZLE 11

NUMBERS USED:
(1-9) 1, 2, 3, 4,
5, 6, 7, 8, 9

20

13

19

6

9

18

PUZZLE 12

14

5

12

NUMBERS USED: (1-7)
1, 2, 3, 4, 5, 6, 7

13

SOLVING SANGAKU™ "RISING SUN" NUMBER PUZZLES

Rising Sun Puzzle designs consist of arching curved lines (3-6). Circles are randomly placed between these curved lines. Lines radiate outward from the center of the design forming pie-shaped figures (see below). Numbers are located at the bottom of the arches. These numbers represent the sum of all the numbers in that particular arch. Numbers located at the outer edge of each pie shape represent the sum of all the numbers in that particular pie shape. To solve these puzzles one must place a given set of numbers correctly to arrive at the sums shown on the puzzle. Place one number in each circle. Below is a sample puzzle and the answer.

SAMPLE PUZZLE

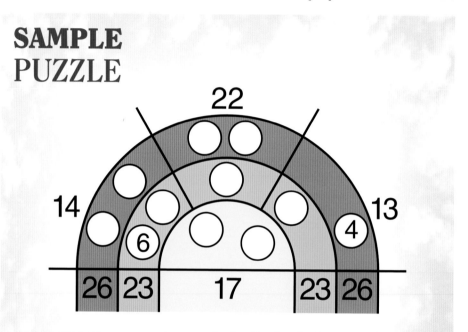

USE THE NUMBERS: (1-11) 1, 2, 3, 4, 5, 6, 7, 8, 9, 10, 11

ANSWER

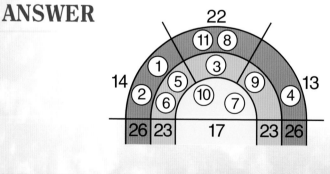

NOTE: ALMOST ALL PUZZLES HAVE MORE THAN ONE SOLUTION.

PUZZLE
1

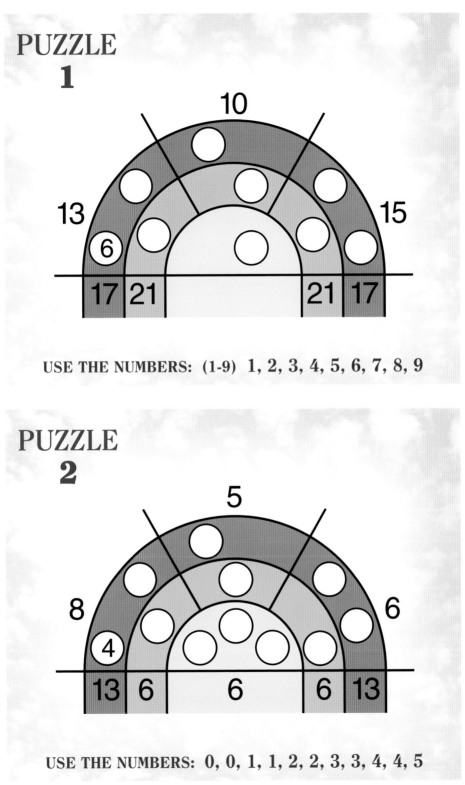

USE THE NUMBERS: (1-9) 1, 2, 3, 4, 5, 6, 7, 8, 9

PUZZLE
2

USE THE NUMBERS: 0, 0, 1, 1, 2, 2, 3, 3, 4, 4, 5

DIRECTIONS FOR SOLVING ARE ON PAGE 40   ANSWERS ON PAGE 122

PUZZLE 3

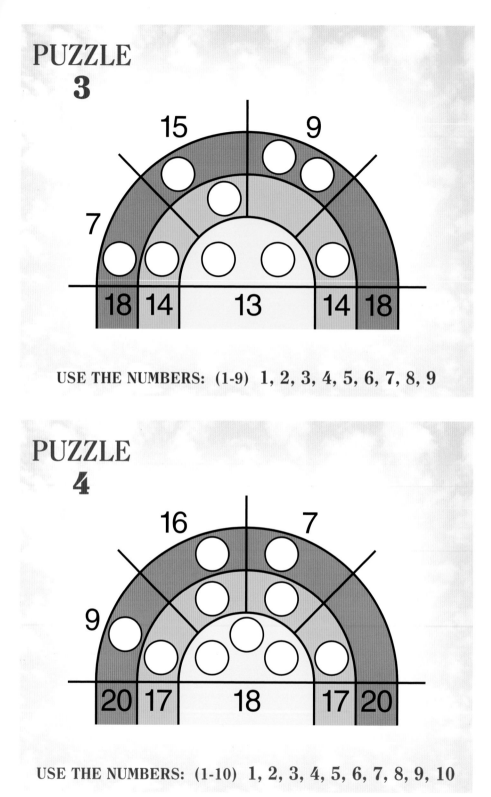

15   9

7

18 | 14 | 13 | 14 | 18

USE THE NUMBERS: (1-9) 1, 2, 3, 4, 5, 6, 7, 8, 9

PUZZLE 4

16   7

9

20 | 17 | 18 | 17 | 20

USE THE NUMBERS: (1-10) 1, 2, 3, 4, 5, 6, 7, 8, 9, 10

DIRECTIONS FOR SOLVING ARE ON PAGE 40   ANSWERS ON PAGE 122

PUZZLE 5

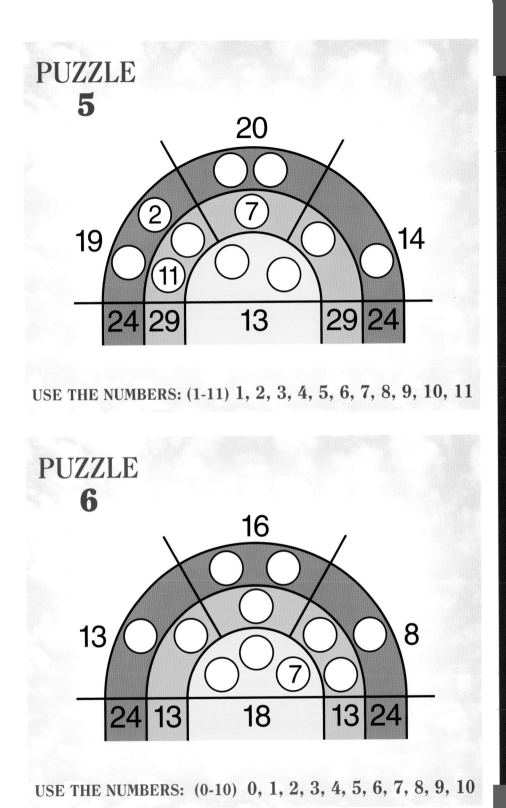

USE THE NUMBERS: (1-11) 1, 2, 3, 4, 5, 6, 7, 8, 9, 10, 11

PUZZLE 6

USE THE NUMBERS: (0-10) 0, 1, 2, 3, 4, 5, 6, 7, 8, 9, 10

DIRECTIONS FOR SOLVING ARE ON PAGE 40   ANSWERS ON PAGE 122

PUZZLE 7

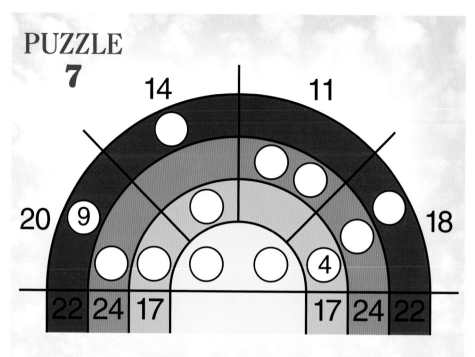

USE THE NUMBERS: (1-12) 1, 2, 3, 4, 5, 6, 7, 8, 9, 10, 11, 12

PUZZLE 8

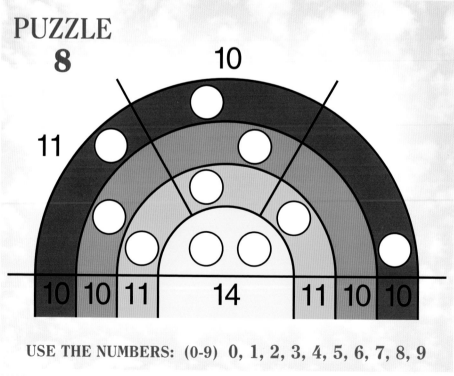

USE THE NUMBERS: (0-9) 0, 1, 2, 3, 4, 5, 6, 7, 8, 9

DIRECTIONS FOR SOLVING ARE ON PAGE 40   ANSWERS ON PAGE 122

PUZZLE 9

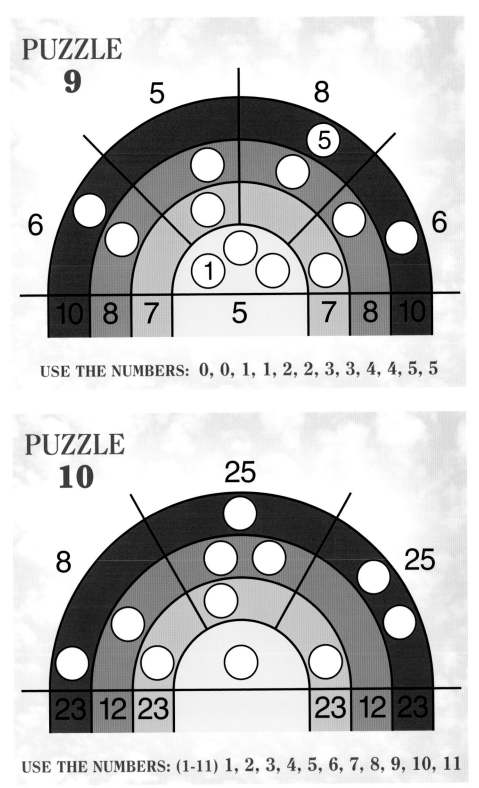

USE THE NUMBERS: 0, 0, 1, 1, 2, 2, 3, 3, 4, 4, 5, 5

PUZZLE 10

USE THE NUMBERS: (1-11) 1, 2, 3, 4, 5, 6, 7, 8, 9, 10, 11

DIRECTIONS FOR SOLVING ARE ON PAGE 40   ANSWERS ON PAGE 122

PUZZLE 11

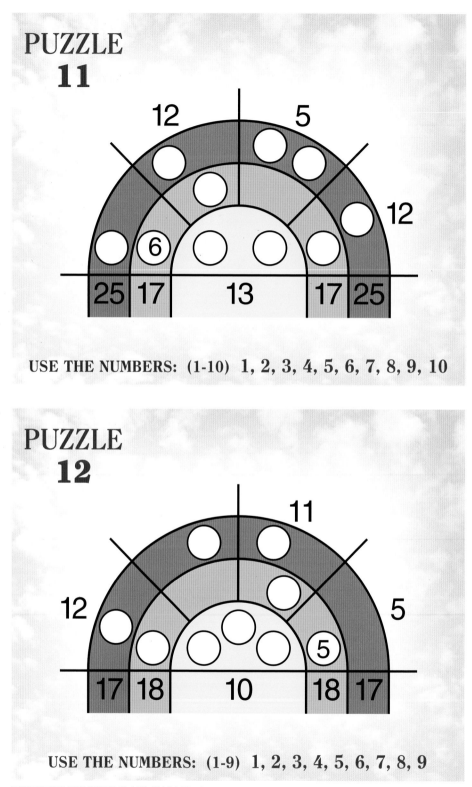

USE THE NUMBERS: (1-10) 1, 2, 3, 4, 5, 6, 7, 8, 9, 10

PUZZLE 12

USE THE NUMBERS: (1-9) 1, 2, 3, 4, 5, 6, 7, 8, 9

DIRECTIONS FOR SOLVING ARE ON PAGE 40   ANSWERS ON PAGE 122

SOLVING SANGAKU™ "NUMBER SELECT" NUMBER PUZZLES

Number Select Puzzles consist of two rectangles, each containing a set of numbers. There are two columns of squares under each rectangle. To the right and bottom of these squares are circles which contain numbers. These numbers represent the sum of all the numbers in that particular row or column. To solve these puzzles one must select numbers from the rectangle above and place them correctly in the squares to get the desired sums. The numbers in the left two columns must be selected from the above left rectangle and the numbers in the right two columns must be selected from the above right rectangle. Do not place numbers in the shaded squares. There are more numbers than needed, so select carefully. Do not use any number more than once.

Below is a sample puzzle with the answer.

NOTE: ALMOST ALL PUZZLES HAVE MORE THAN ONE SOLUTION.

PUZZLE **1**

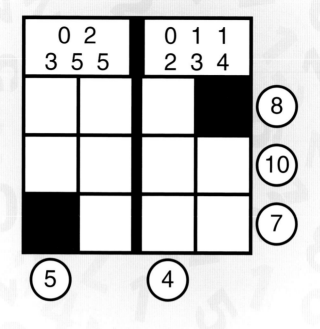

PUZZLE **2**

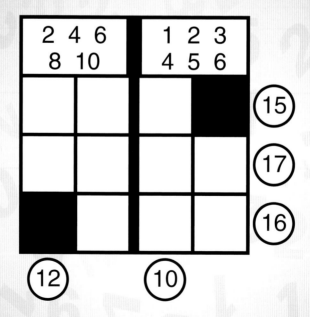

PUZZLE 3

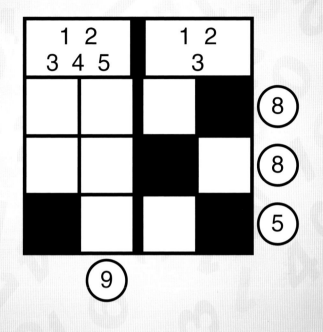

PUZZLE 4

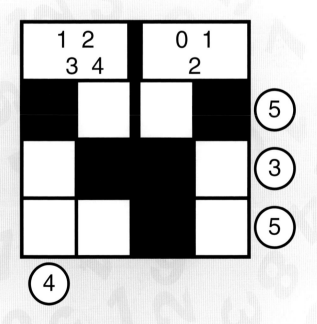

PUZZLE **5**

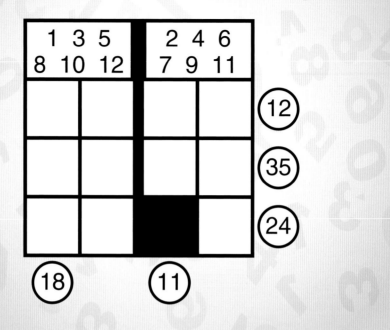

PUZZLE **6**

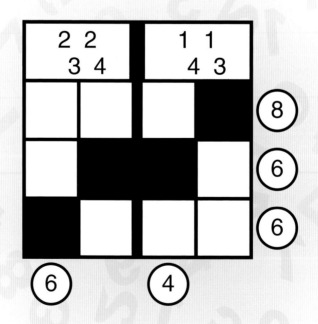

PUZZLE **7**

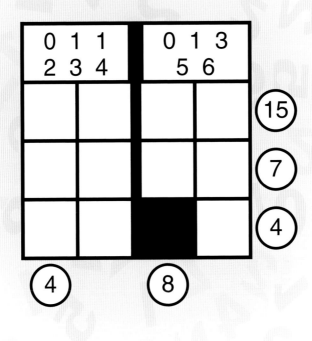

PUZZLE **8**

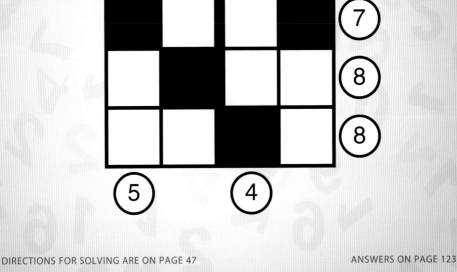

DIRECTIONS FOR SOLVING ARE ON PAGE 47

ANSWERS ON PAGE 123

PUZZLE **9**

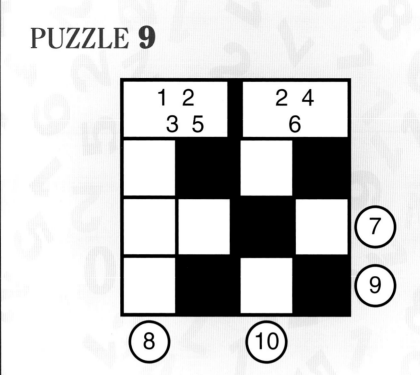

1 2 3 5	2 4 6

⑦
⑨

⑧ ⑩

PUZZLE **10**

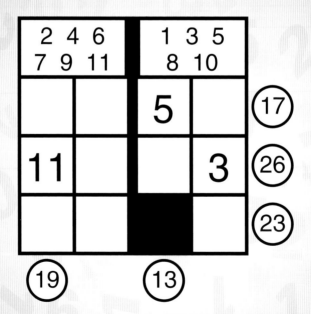

2 4 6 7 9 11	1 3 5 8 10

5 ⑰
11 **3** ㉖
㉓

⑲ ⑬

PUZZLE 11

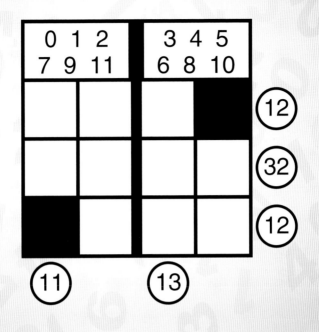

PUZZLE 12

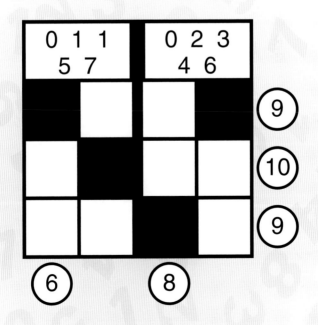

SOLVING SANGAKU™ "HORSESHOE" NUMBER PUZZLES

These puzzles consist of circles randomly placed inside horseshoe shapes (4-8) pointing upward and pointing downward. A number at the bottom of a downward pointing horseshoe represents the sum of all the numbers in that particular horseshoe. A number at the top of an upward pointing horseshoe represents the sum of all the numbers inside that horseshoe. To solve these puzzles, a given set of numbers must be correctly placed in the circles so that all sums are as shown. Use each number only once. Below are two sample puzzles with answers.

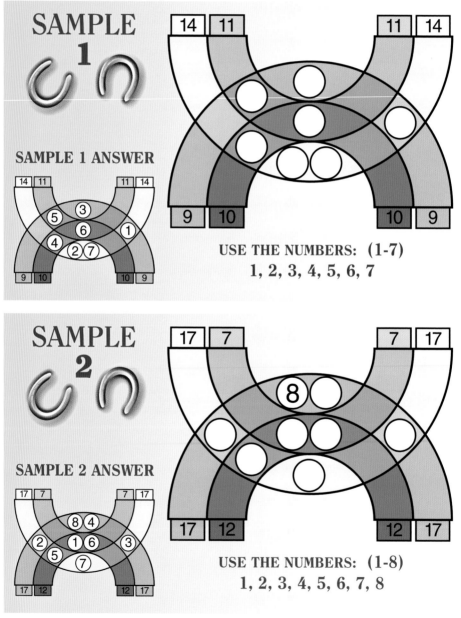

SAMPLE **1**

SAMPLE 1 ANSWER

USE THE NUMBERS: (1-7)
1, 2, 3, 4, 5, 6, 7

SAMPLE **2**

SAMPLE 2 ANSWER

USE THE NUMBERS: (1-8)
1, 2, 3, 4, 5, 6, 7, 8

NOTE: ALMOST ALL PUZZLES HAVE MORE THAN ONE SOLUTION.

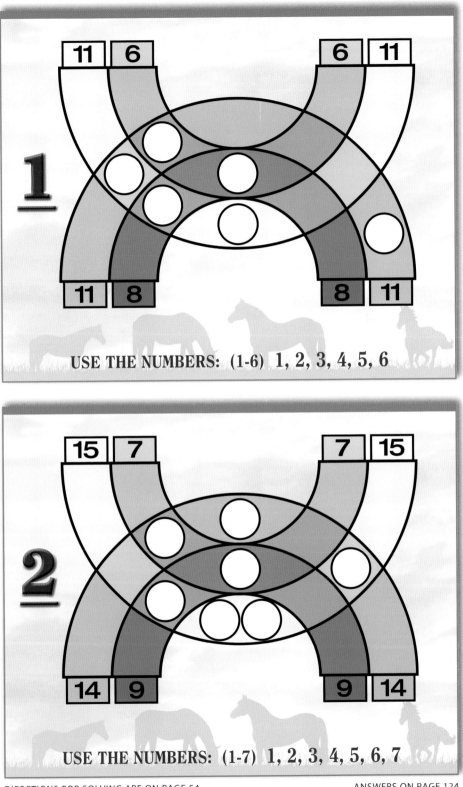

1

| 11 | 6 | | 6 | 11 |

| 11 | 8 | | 8 | 11 |

USE THE NUMBERS: (1-6) 1, 2, 3, 4, 5, 6

2

| 15 | 7 | | 7 | 15 |

| 14 | 9 | | 9 | 14 |

USE THE NUMBERS: (1-7) 1, 2, 3, 4, 5, 6, 7

DIRECTIONS FOR SOLVING ARE ON PAGE 54

ANSWERS ON PAGE 124

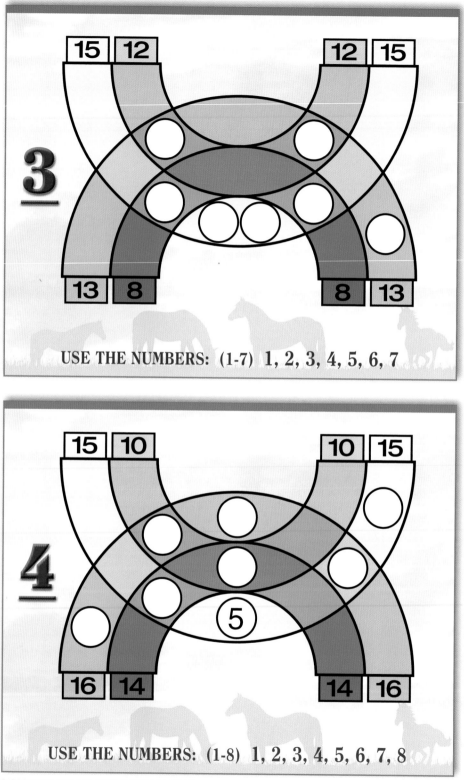

3

15 12   12 15

13 8   8 13

USE THE NUMBERS: (1-7) 1, 2, 3, 4, 5, 6, 7

4

15 10   10 15

5

16 14   14 16

USE THE NUMBERS: (1-8) 1, 2, 3, 4, 5, 6, 7, 8

DIRECTIONS FOR SOLVING ARE ON PAGE 54 ANSWERS ON PAGE 124

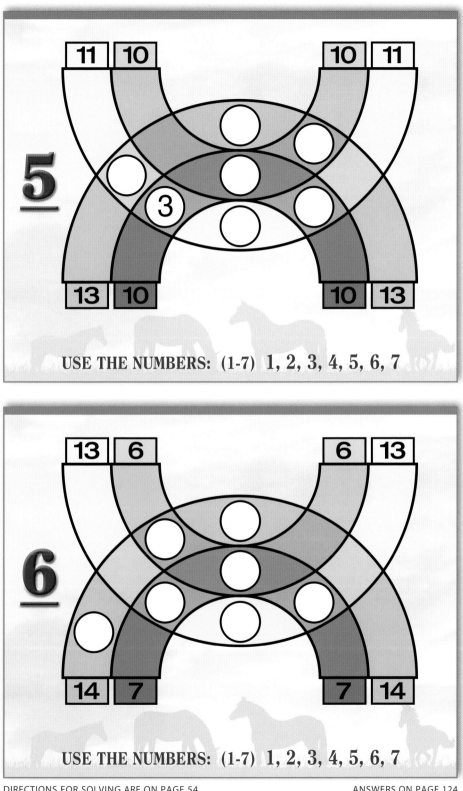

USE THE NUMBERS: (1-7) 1, 2, 3, 4, 5, 6, 7

USE THE NUMBERS: (1-7) 1, 2, 3, 4, 5, 6, 7

DIRECTIONS FOR SOLVING ARE ON PAGE 54

ANSWERS ON PAGE 124

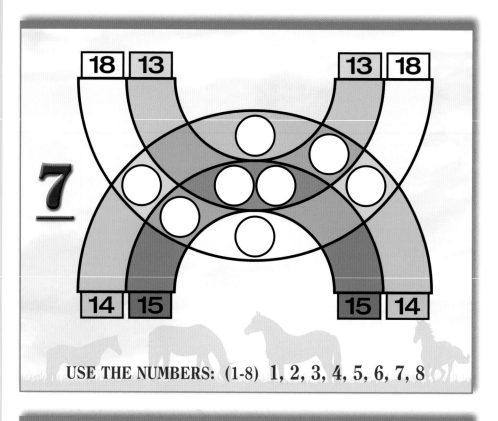

7

USE THE NUMBERS: (1-8) 1, 2, 3, 4, 5, 6, 7, 8

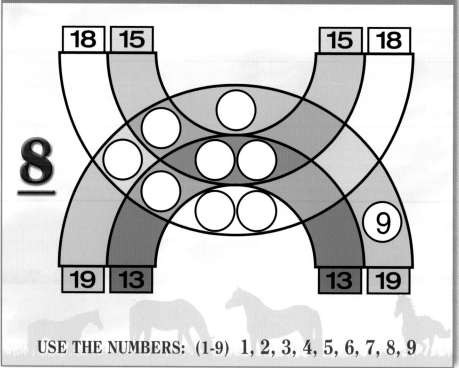

8

USE THE NUMBERS: (1-9) 1, 2, 3, 4, 5, 6, 7, 8, 9

SOLVING SANGAKU™ "X" FACTOR NUMBER PUZZLES

"X" Factor Number Puzzles always contain an "x." There may be any number of "x"(s) in a puzzle design. The "x"(s) may be adjacent to one another or placed on a circle, square, or other geometric figure. At the end of each line of squares that form the "x" are numbers. These numbers represent the sum of all the numbers to be placed in that particular row. Beside each puzzle is a "hint" — a miniature section of the puzzle followed by a number. This number represents the sum of all the numbers in the blank spaces in that miniature section. To solve each puzzle, place a given set of numbers in the spaces to arrive at the sums shown. Do not place numbers in the shaded areas. Below is a sample puzzle with the answer.

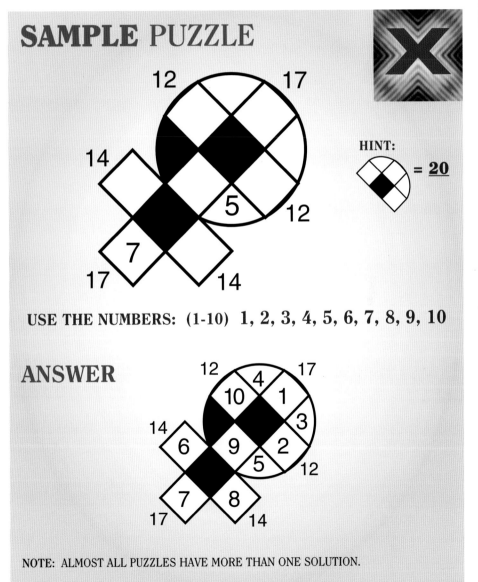

USE THE NUMBERS: (1-10) 1, 2, 3, 4, 5, 6, 7, 8, 9, 10

NOTE: ALMOST ALL PUZZLES HAVE MORE THAN ONE SOLUTION.

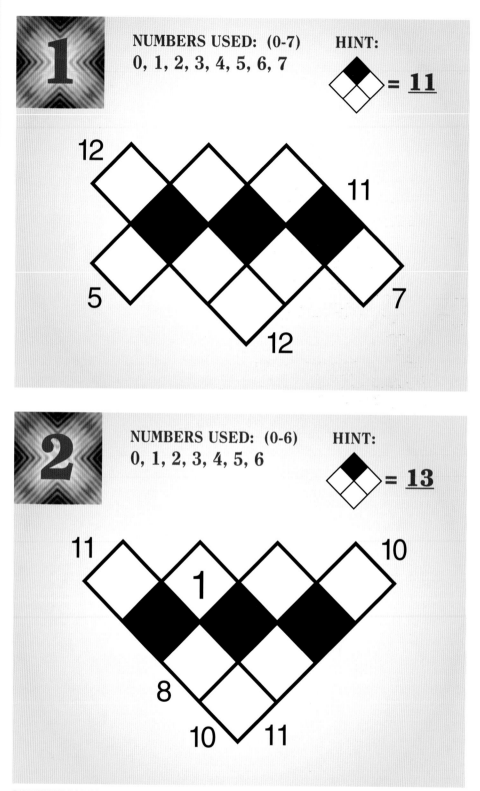

1

NUMBERS USED: (0-7)
0, 1, 2, 3, 4, 5, 6, 7

HINT:
= **11**

12

11

5

7

12

2

NUMBERS USED: (0-6)
0, 1, 2, 3, 4, 5, 6

HINT:
= **13**

11

1

10

8

10

11

DIRECTIONS FOR SOLVING ARE ON PAGE 59

ANSWERS ON PAGE 125

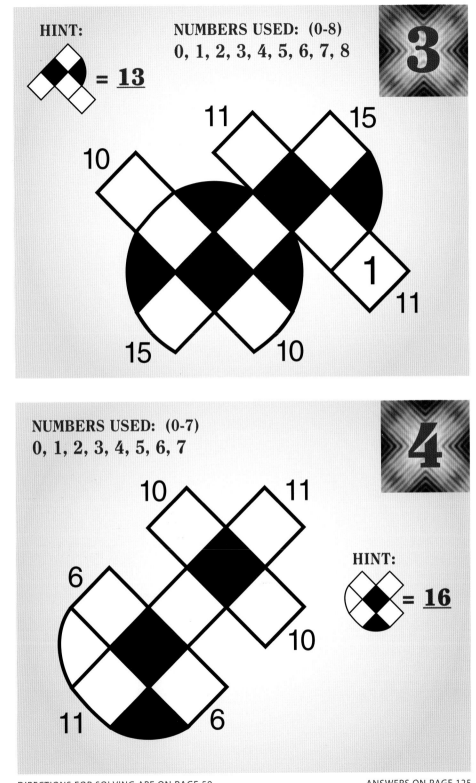

HINT:

= **13**

NUMBERS USED: (0-8)
0, 1, 2, 3, 4, 5, 6, 7, 8

3

11   15

10

1

11

15   10

NUMBERS USED: (0-7)
0, 1, 2, 3, 4, 5, 6, 7

4

10   11

6

HINT:

= **16**

10

11   6

5

HINT:

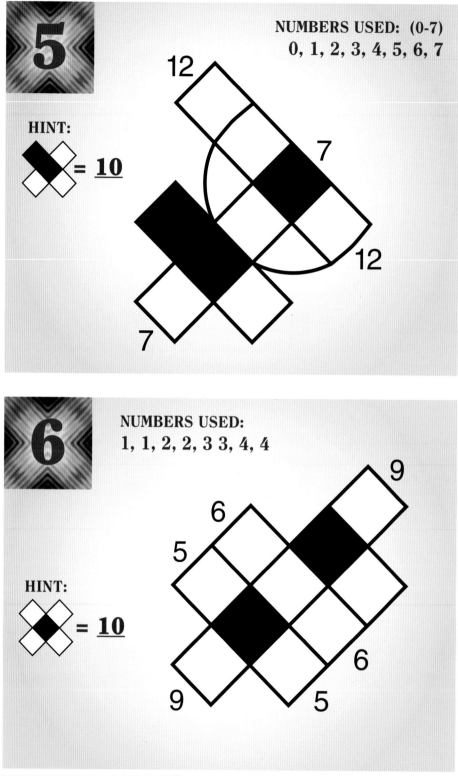

= **10**

12

7

12

7

6

NUMBERS USED:
1, 1, 2, 2, 3 3, 4, 4

9

6

5

6

9

5

HINT:

= **10**

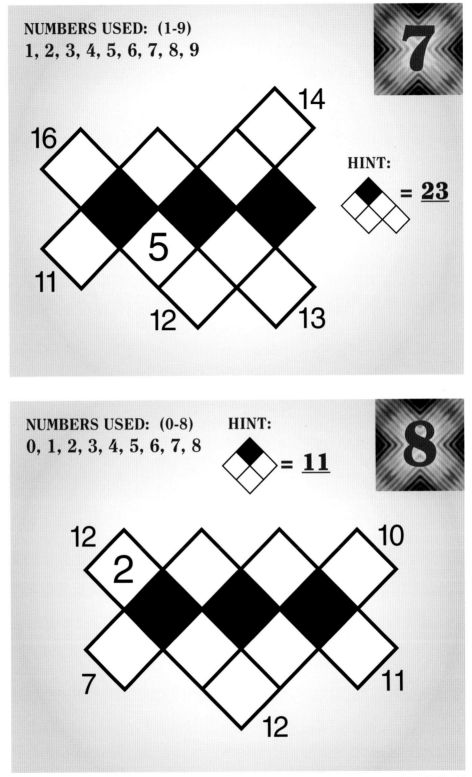

NUMBERS USED: (1-9)
1, 2, 3, 4, 5, 6, 7, 8, 9

14

16

HINT:

■ = **23**

5

11

12   13

NUMBERS USED: (0-8)
0, 1, 2, 3, 4, 5, 6, 7, 8

HINT:

■ = **11**

12   2   10

7   11

12

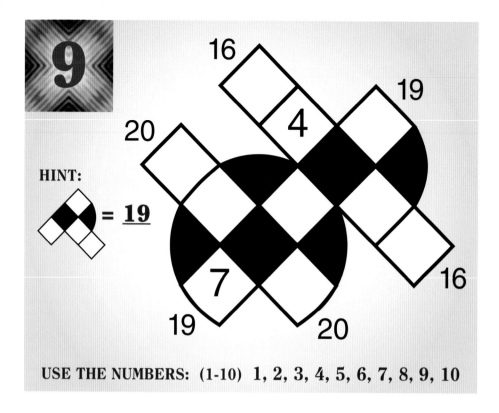

9

HINT:

= **19**

USE THE NUMBERS: (1-10) 1, 2, 3, 4, 5, 6, 7, 8, 9, 10

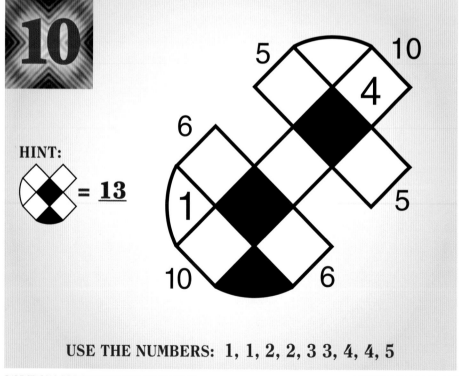

10

HINT:

= **13**

USE THE NUMBERS: 1, 1, 2, 2, 3 3, 4, 4, 5

NUMBERS USED: (1-8)
1, 2, 3, 4, 5, 6, 7, 8

11

HINT:

= **16**

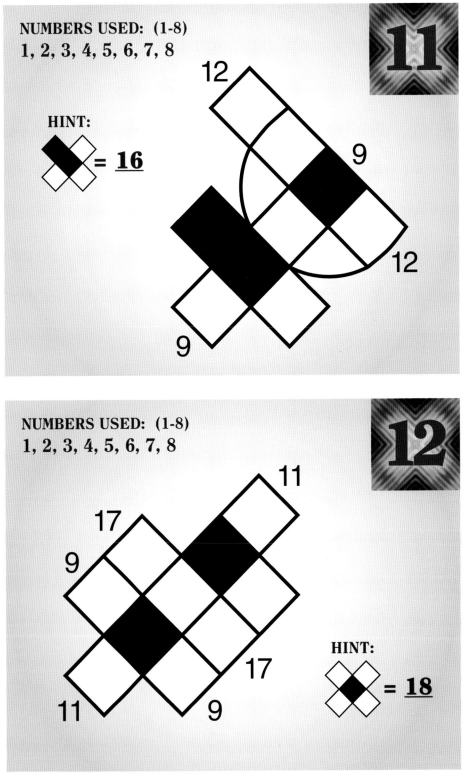

12

9

12

9

NUMBERS USED: (1-8)
1, 2, 3, 4, 5, 6, 7, 8

12

11

17

9

17

9

11

HINT:

= **18**

Professor Hill™ invites you to try your skill
at these *more challenging* number puzzles.

TOUGH
DECISIONS
AHEAD

MORE
CHALLENGING
NUMBER
PUZZLES
→

PUZZLE 1

NUMBERS USED: (0-8)
0, 1, 2, 3, 4, 5, 6, 7, 8

SUM OF **12**

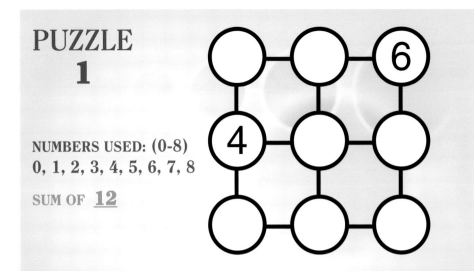

These four = 12   These four = 12   These four = 12   These four = 12

PUZZLE 2

NUMBERS USED: (1-8)
1, 2, 3, 4, 5, 6, 7, 8

SUM OF **18**

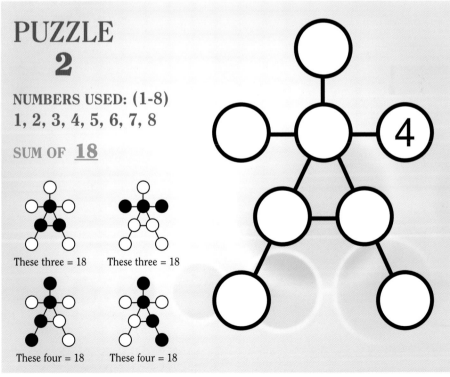

These three = 18   These three = 18

These four = 18   These four = 18

DIRECTIONS FOR SOLVING ARE ON PAGE 8

ANSWERS ON PAGE 126

PUZZLE 3

NUMBERS USED: (0-7)
0, 1, 2, 3, 4, 5, 6, 7

SUM OF **16**

These four = 16   These four = 16

These four = 16

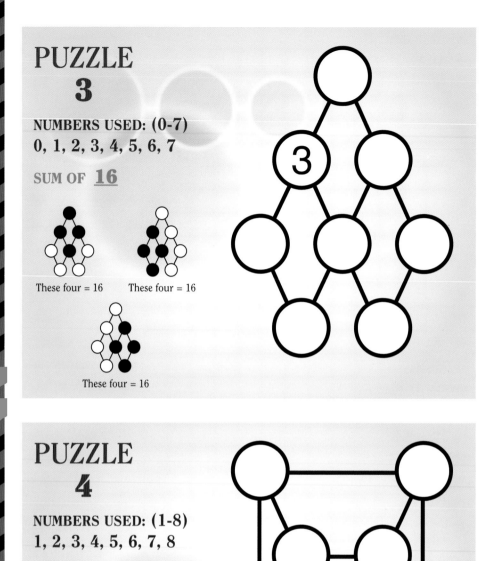

PUZZLE 4

NUMBERS USED: (1-8)
1, 2, 3, 4, 5, 6, 7, 8

SUM OF **18**

These four = 18   These four = 18

These four = 18   These four = 18

DIRECTIONS FOR SOLVING ARE ON PAGE 8   ANSWERS ON PAGE 126

PUZZLE 5

NUMBERS USED: (1-8)
1, 2, 3, 4, 5, 6, 7, 8

SUM OF **14**

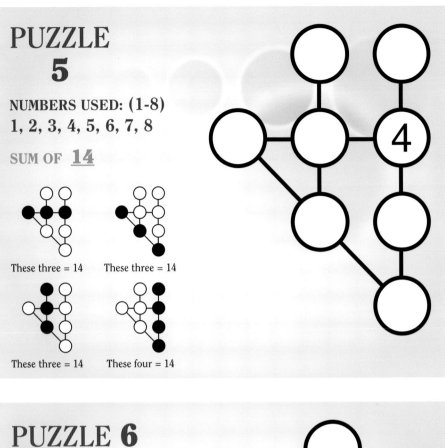

These three = 14   These three = 14

These three = 14   These four = 14

PUZZLE 6

NUMBERS USED: (1-8)
1, 2, 3, 4, 5, 6, 7, 8

SUM OF **18**

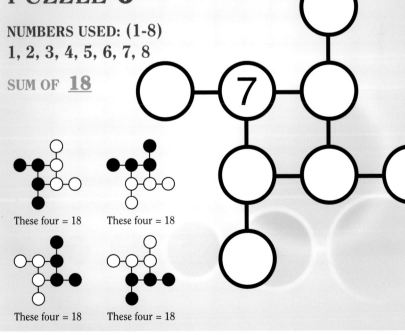

These four = 18   These four = 18

These four = 18   These four = 18

DIRECTIONS FOR SOLVING ARE ON PAGE 8   ANSWERS ON PAGE 126

PUZZLE 7

NUMBERS USED: (1-10)
1, 2, 3, 4, 5,
6, 7, 8, 9, 10

SUM OF **22**

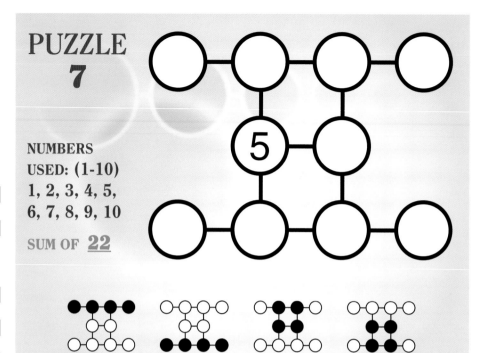

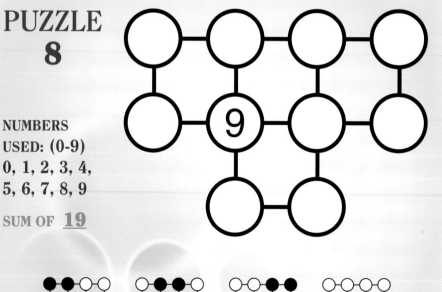

These four = 22   These four = 22   These four = 22   These four = 22

PUZZLE 8

NUMBERS USED: (0-9)
0, 1, 2, 3, 4,
5, 6, 7, 8, 9

SUM OF **19**

These four = 19   These four = 19   These four = 19   These four = 19

DIRECTIONS FOR SOLVING ARE ON PAGE 8   ANSWERS ON PAGE 126

PUZZLE 9

NUMBERS USED: (1-8)
1, 2, 3, 4, 5, 6, 7, 8

SUM OF **16**

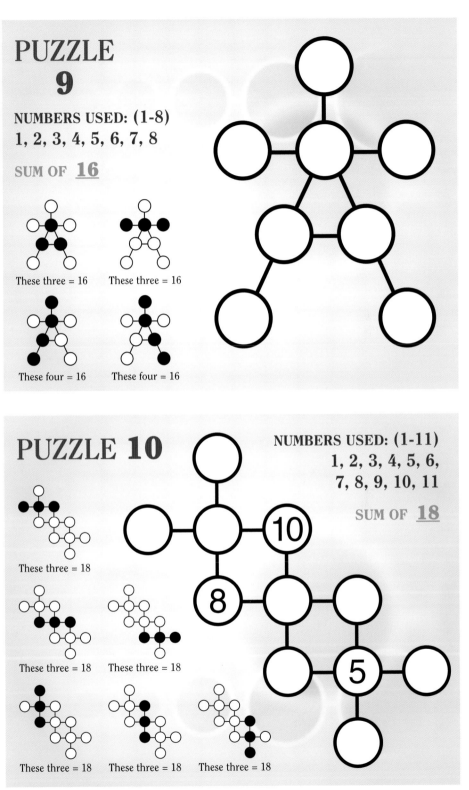

These three = 16

These three = 16

These four = 16

These four = 16

PUZZLE 10

NUMBERS USED: (1-11)
1, 2, 3, 4, 5, 6,
7, 8, 9, 10, 11

SUM OF **18**

These three = 18

These three = 18

These three = 18

These three = 18

These three = 18

These three = 18

DIRECTIONS FOR SOLVING ARE ON PAGE 8

ANSWERS ON PAGE 126

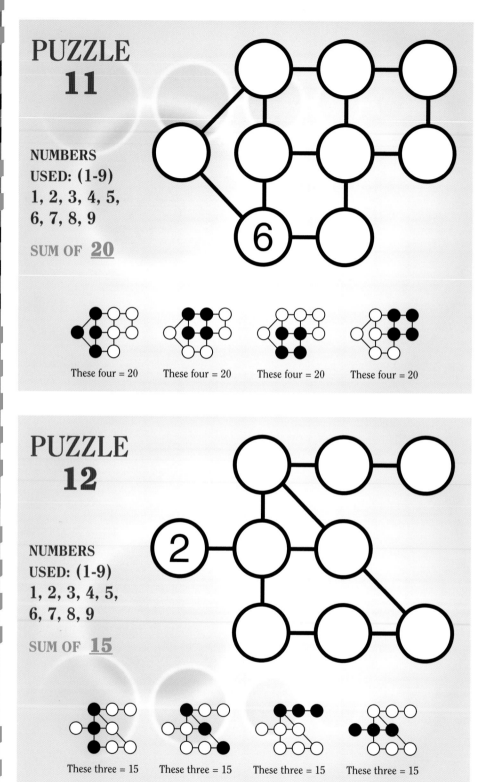

PUZZLE 11

NUMBERS USED: (1-9)
1, 2, 3, 4, 5, 6, 7, 8, 9

SUM OF **20**

These four = 20   These four = 20   These four = 20   These four = 20

PUZZLE 12

NUMBERS USED: (1-9)
1, 2, 3, 4, 5, 6, 7, 8, 9

SUM OF **15**

These three = 15   These three = 15   These three = 15   These three = 15

PUZZLE 13

NUMBERS USED: (1-9)
1, 2, 3, 4, 5, 6, 7, 8, 9

SUM OF **18**

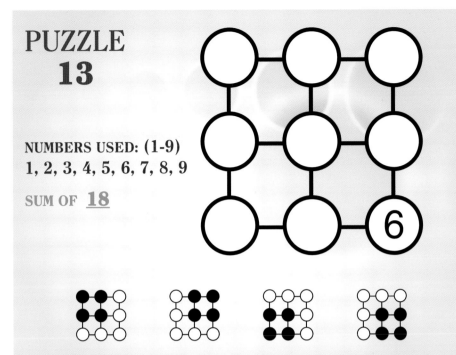

| These four = 18 | These four = 18 | These four = 18 | These four = 18 |

PUZZLE 14

NUMBERS USED:
1, 1, 2, 2, 3, 3, 4, 4

SUM OF **10**

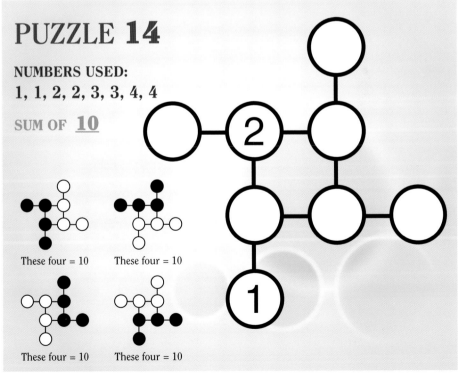

These four = 10 These four = 10

These four = 10 These four = 10

DIRECTIONS FOR SOLVING ARE ON PAGE 8   ANSWERS ON PAGE 126

PUZZLE 15

NUMBERS USED: (1-9)
1, 2, 3, 4, 5, 6, 7, 8, 9

SUM OF **16**

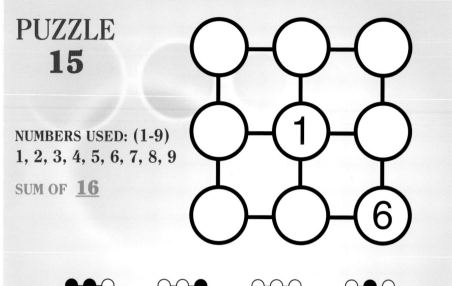

These four = 16   These four = 16   These four = 16   These four = 16

PUZZLE 16

NUMBERS USED: (0-7)
0, 1, 2, 3, 4, 5, 6, 7

SUM OF **12**

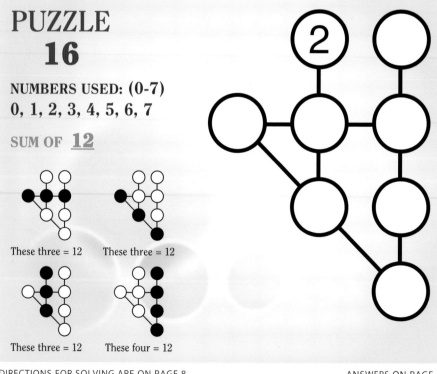

These three = 12   These three = 12

These three = 12   These four = 12

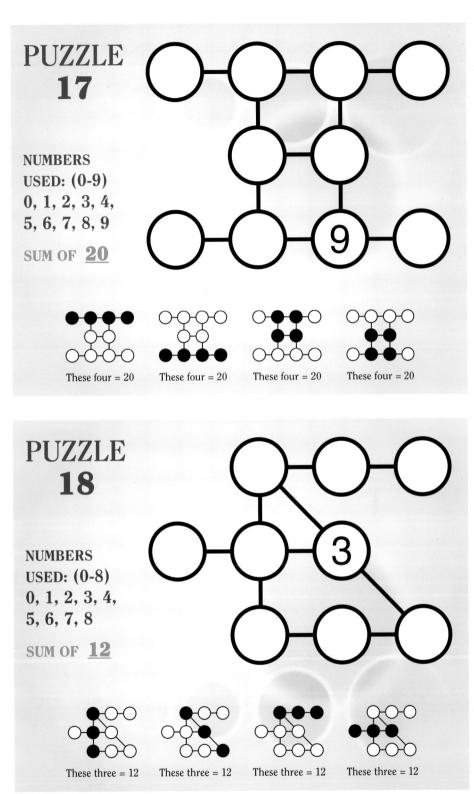

PUZZLE 17

NUMBERS USED: (0-9)
0, 1, 2, 3, 4, 5, 6, 7, 8, 9

SUM OF **20**

These four = 20 | These four = 20 | These four = 20 | These four = 20

PUZZLE 18

NUMBERS USED: (0-8)
0, 1, 2, 3, 4, 5, 6, 7, 8

SUM OF **12**

These three = 12 | These three = 12 | These three = 12 | These three = 12

DIRECTIONS FOR SOLVING ARE ON PAGE 8

ANSWERS ON PAGE 127

PUZZLE 19

NUMBERS USED:
1, 1, 2, 2, 3, 3, 4, 4, 5, 5

SUM OF **13**

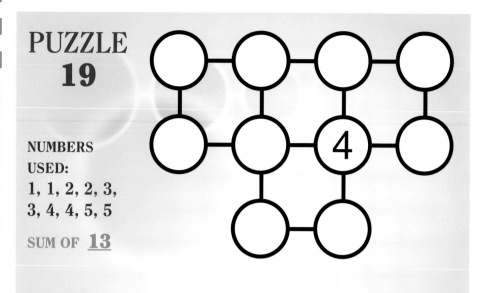

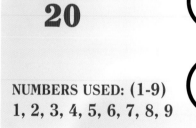

These four = 13   These four = 13   These four = 13   These four = 13

PUZZLE 20

NUMBERS USED: (1-9)
1, 2, 3, 4, 5, 6, 7, 8, 9

SUM OF **19**

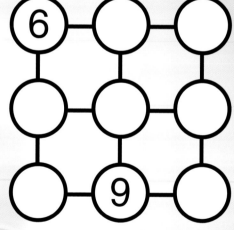

These four = 19   These four = 19   These four = 19   These four = 19

DIRECTIONS FOR SOLVING ARE ON PAGE 8   ANSWERS ON PAGE 127

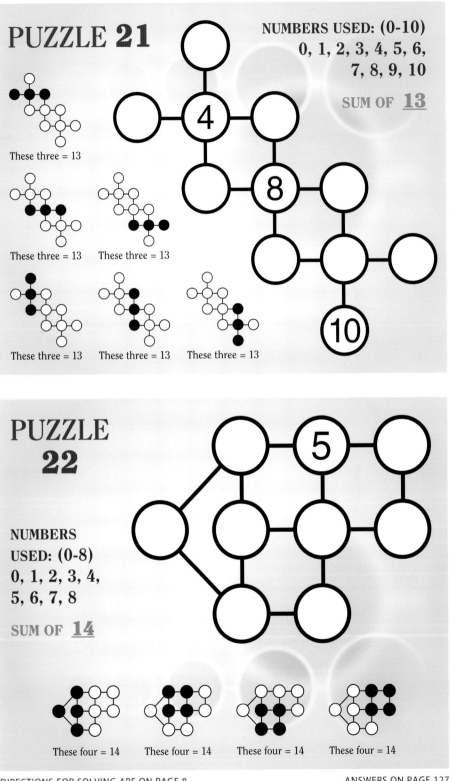

PUZZLE 21

NUMBERS USED: (0-10)
0, 1, 2, 3, 4, 5, 6,
7, 8, 9, 10

SUM OF **13**

These three = 13

These three = 13   These three = 13

These three = 13   These three = 13   These three = 13

PUZZLE 22

NUMBERS
USED: (0-8)
0, 1, 2, 3, 4,
5, 6, 7, 8

SUM OF **14**

These four = 14   These four = 14   These four = 14   These four = 14

DIRECTIONS FOR SOLVING ARE ON PAGE 8   ANSWERS ON PAGE 127

PUZZLE 1

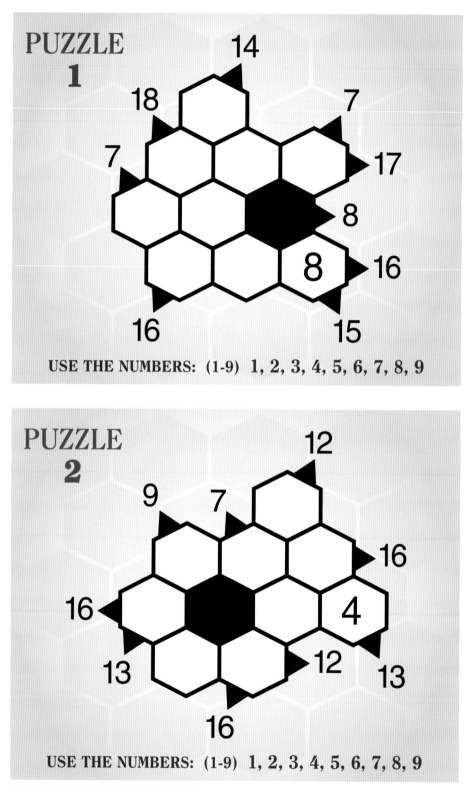

14 18 7 7 17 8 8 16 16 15

USE THE NUMBERS: (1-9) 1, 2, 3, 4, 5, 6, 7, 8, 9

PUZZLE 2

12 9 7 16 16 4 13 12 13 16

USE THE NUMBERS: (1-9) 1, 2, 3, 4, 5, 6, 7, 8, 9

DIRECTIONS FOR SOLVING ARE ON PAGE 20   ANSWERS ON PAGE 127

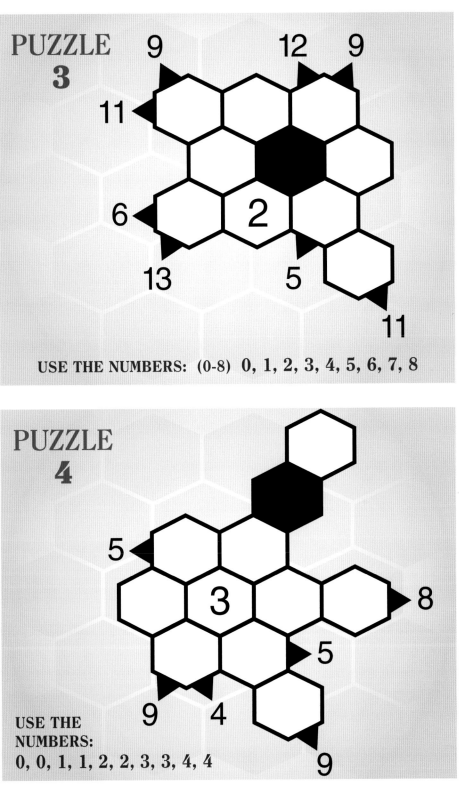

PUZZLE 3

9   12   9

11

6

2

13   5

11

USE THE NUMBERS: (0-8) **0, 1, 2, 3, 4, 5, 6, 7, 8**

PUZZLE 4

5

3

8

5

9   4

9

USE THE NUMBERS:
0, 0, 1, 1, 2, 2, 3, 3, 4, 4

DIRECTIONS FOR SOLVING ARE ON PAGE 20   ANSWERS ON PAGE 127

PUZZLE 5

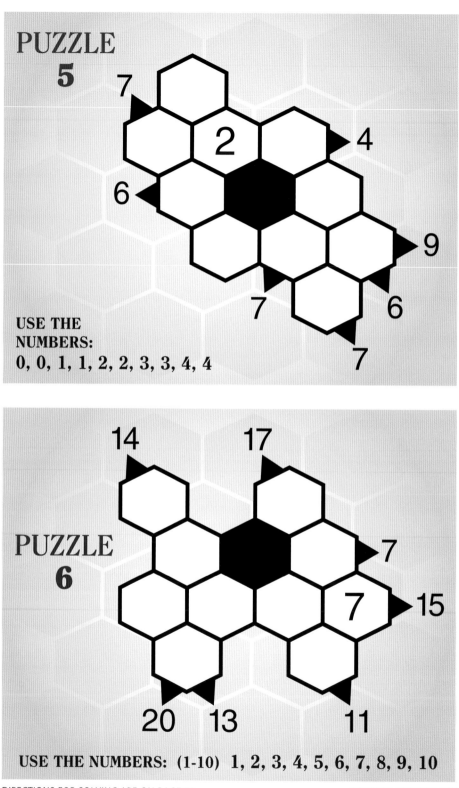

USE THE
NUMBERS:
0, 0, 1, 1, 2, 2, 3, 3, 4, 4

PUZZLE 6

USE THE NUMBERS: (1-10) 1, 2, 3, 4, 5, 6, 7, 8, 9, 10

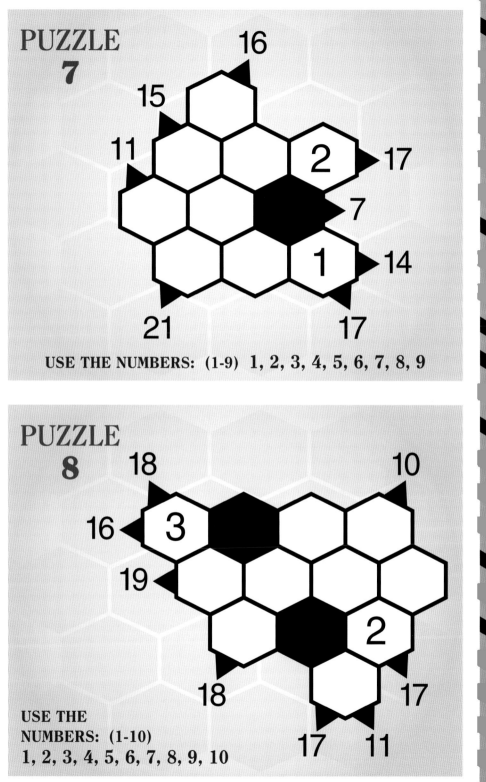

PUZZLE 7

16
15
11
2
17
7
1
14
21
17

USE THE NUMBERS: (1-9) 1, 2, 3, 4, 5, 6, 7, 8, 9

PUZZLE 8

18
10
16
3
19
2
18
17
17
11

USE THE
NUMBERS: (1-10)
1, 2, 3, 4, 5, 6, 7, 8, 9, 10

DIRECTIONS FOR SOLVING ARE ON PAGE 20   ANSWERS ON PAGE 127

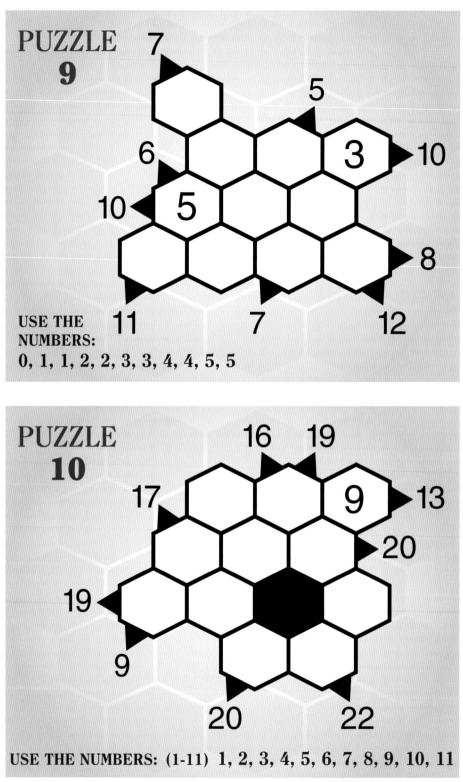

PUZZLE 9

USE THE NUMBERS:
0, 1, 1, 2, 2, 3, 3, 4, 4, 5, 5

PUZZLE 10

USE THE NUMBERS: (1-11) 1, 2, 3, 4, 5, 6, 7, 8, 9, 10, 11

DIRECTIONS FOR SOLVING ARE ON PAGE 20   ANSWERS ON PAGE 128

PUZZLE 11

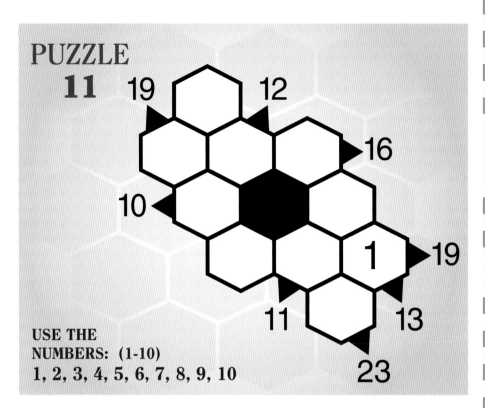

USE THE NUMBERS: (1-10)
1, 2, 3, 4, 5, 6, 7, 8, 9, 10

PUZZLE 12

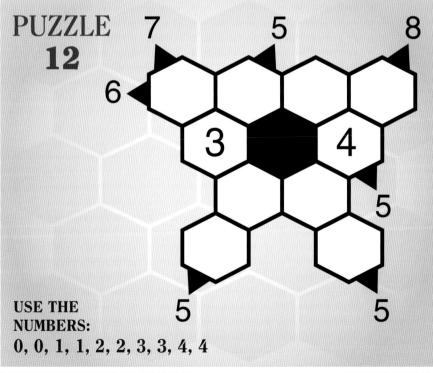

USE THE NUMBERS:
0, 0, 1, 1, 2, 2, 3, 3, 4, 4

DIRECTIONS FOR SOLVING ARE ON PAGE 20

ANSWERS ON PAGE 128

PUZZLE 13

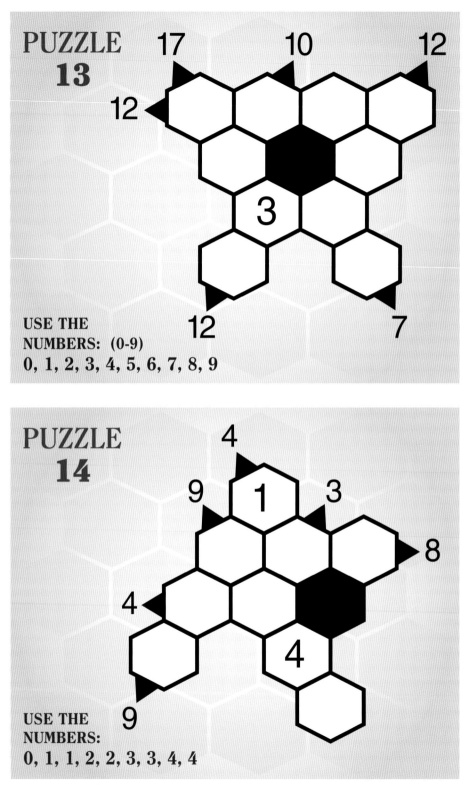

USE THE
NUMBERS: (0-9)
0, 1, 2, 3, 4, 5, 6, 7, 8, 9

PUZZLE 14

USE THE
NUMBERS:
0, 1, 1, 2, 2, 3, 3, 4, 4

DIRECTIONS FOR SOLVING ARE ON PAGE 20   ANSWERS ON PAGE 128

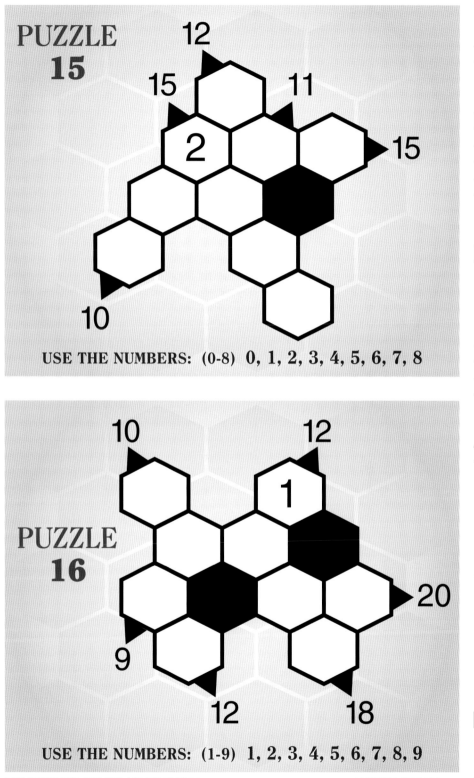

PUZZLE **15**

12

15   11

2   15

10

USE THE NUMBERS: (0-8) 0, 1, 2, 3, 4, 5, 6, 7, 8

PUZZLE **16**

10   12

1

20

9

12   18

USE THE NUMBERS: (1-9) 1, 2, 3, 4, 5, 6, 7, 8, 9

DIRECTIONS FOR SOLVING ARE ON PAGE 20   ANSWERS ON PAGE 128

PUZZLE 17

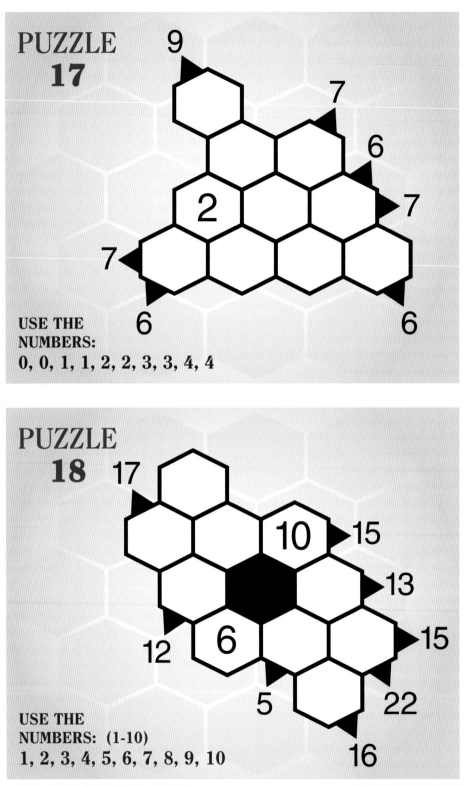

9

7

6

2

7

7

7

6

6

USE THE NUMBERS:
0, 0, 1, 1, 2, 2, 3, 3, 4, 4

PUZZLE 18

17

10

15

13

12

6

15

5

22

16

USE THE NUMBERS: (1-10)
1, 2, 3, 4, 5, 6, 7, 8, 9, 10

PUZZLE 19

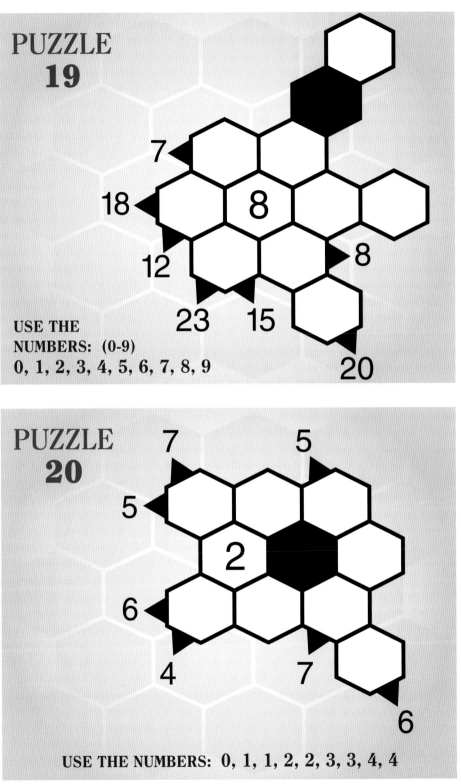

7
18
12
8
8
23 15
20

USE THE
NUMBERS: (0-9)
0, 1, 2, 3, 4, 5, 6, 7, 8, 9

PUZZLE 20

7 5
5
2
6
4 7
6

USE THE NUMBERS: 0, 1, 1, 2, 2, 3, 3, 4, 4

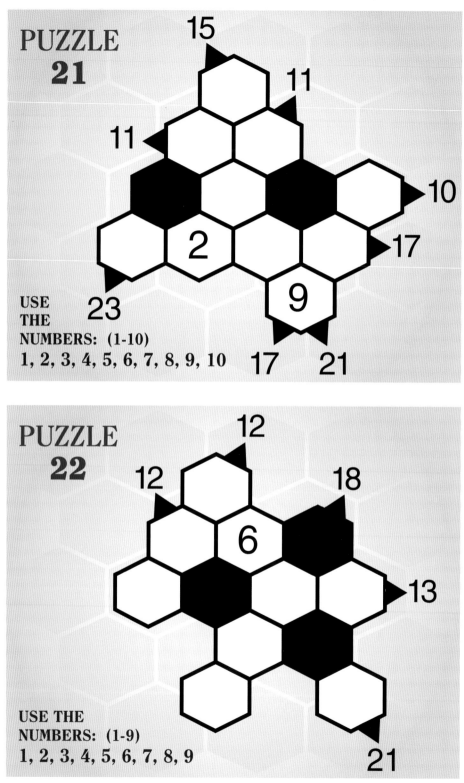

PUZZLE 21

15
11
11
10
2
17
9
23
17   21

USE
THE
NUMBERS: (1-10)
1, 2, 3, 4, 5, 6, 7, 8, 9, 10

PUZZLE 22

12
12
18
6
13
21

USE THE
NUMBERS: (1-9)
1, 2, 3, 4, 5, 6, 7, 8, 9

DIRECTIONS FOR SOLVING ARE ON PAGE 20   ANSWERS ON PAGE 128

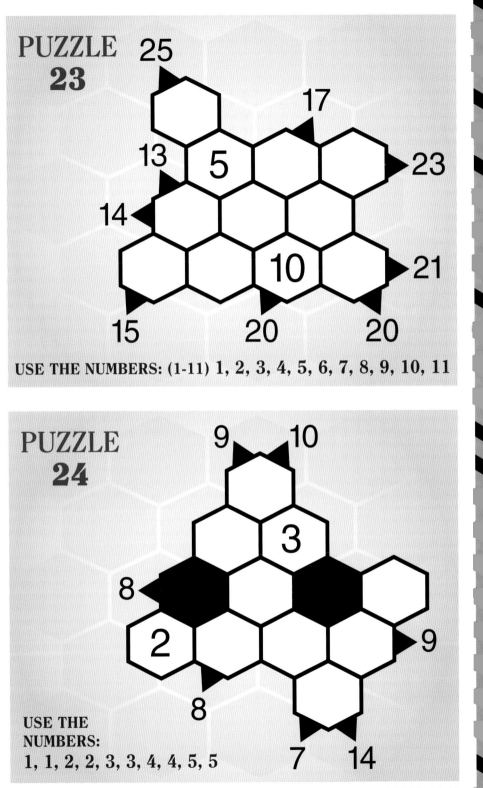

PUZZLE 23

USE THE NUMBERS: (1-11) 1, 2, 3, 4, 5, 6, 7, 8, 9, 10, 11

PUZZLE 24

USE THE NUMBERS:
1, 1, 2, 2, 3, 3, 4, 4, 5, 5

DIRECTIONS FOR SOLVING ARE ON PAGE 20   ANSWERS ON PAGE 128

PUZZLE 1

NUMBERS USED:
0, 1, 2, 2, 3, 3, 4, 5

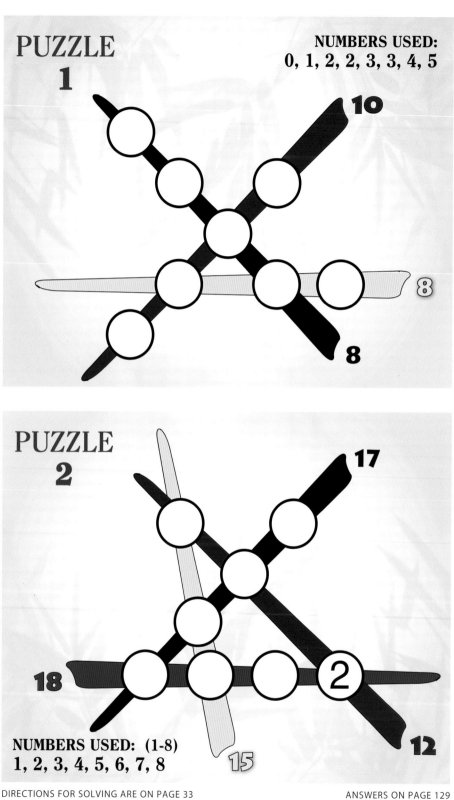

PUZZLE 2

NUMBERS USED: (1-8)
1, 2, 3, 4, 5, 6, 7, 8

DIRECTIONS FOR SOLVING ARE ON PAGE 33

ANSWERS ON PAGE 129

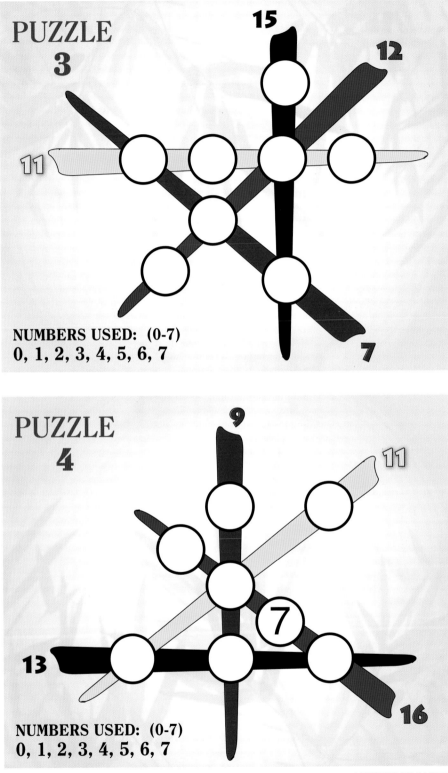

PUZZLE 3

15

12

11

7

NUMBERS USED: (0-7)
0, 1, 2, 3, 4, 5, 6, 7

PUZZLE 4

9

11

7

13

16

NUMBERS USED: (0-7)
0, 1, 2, 3, 4, 5, 6, 7

DIRECTIONS FOR SOLVING ARE ON PAGE 33 ANSWERS ON PAGE 129

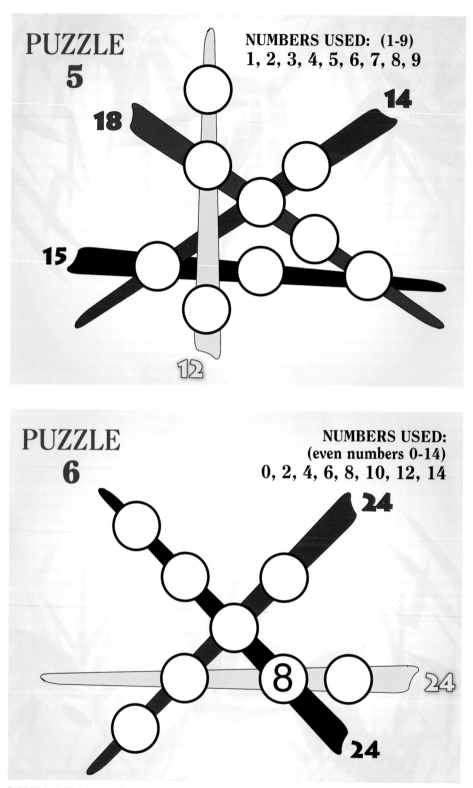

PUZZLE **5**

NUMBERS USED: (1-9)
1, 2, 3, 4, 5, 6, 7, 8, 9

14
18
15
12

PUZZLE **6**

NUMBERS USED:
(even numbers 0-14)
0, 2, 4, 6, 8, 10, 12, 14

24
24
24
8

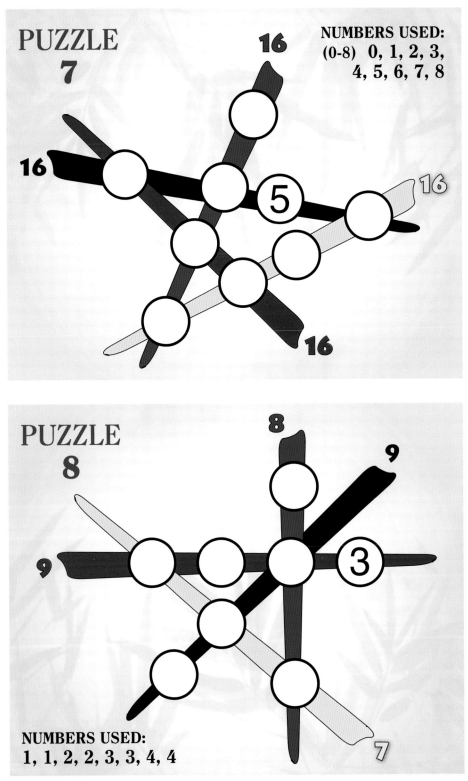

PUZZLE 7

16

NUMBERS USED:
(0-8) 0, 1, 2, 3,
4, 5, 6, 7, 8

16

5

16

16

PUZZLE 8

8

9

9

3

7

NUMBERS USED:
1, 1, 2, 2, 3, 3, 4, 4

DIRECTIONS FOR SOLVING ARE ON PAGE 33

ANSWERS ON PAGE 129

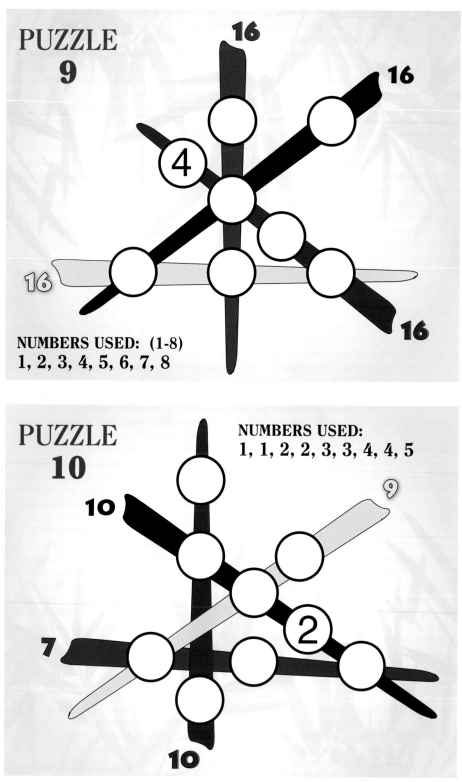

PUZZLE 9

16

16

4

16

16

NUMBERS USED: (1-8)
1, 2, 3, 4, 5, 6, 7, 8

PUZZLE 10

NUMBERS USED:
1, 1, 2, 2, 3, 3, 4, 4, 5

9

10

2

7

10

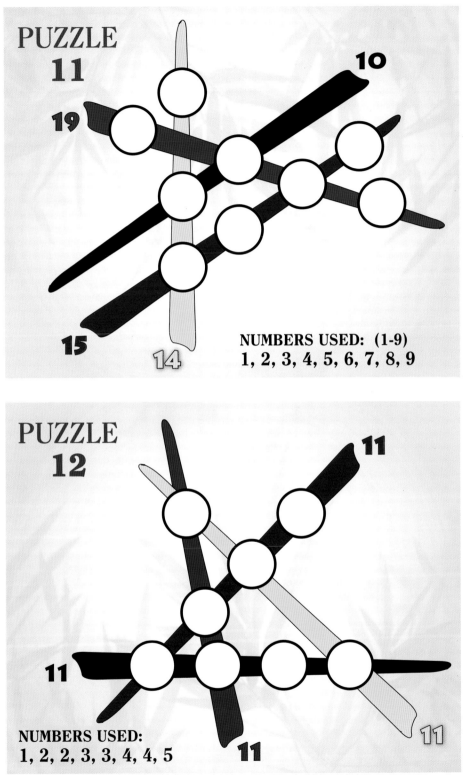

PUZZLE
11

10

19

15

14

NUMBERS USED: (1-9)
1, 2, 3, 4, 5, 6, 7, 8, 9

PUZZLE
12

11

11

11

NUMBERS USED:
1, 2, 2, 3, 3, 4, 4, 5

DIRECTIONS FOR SOLVING ARE ON PAGE 33

ANSWERS ON PAGE 129

PUZZLE 1

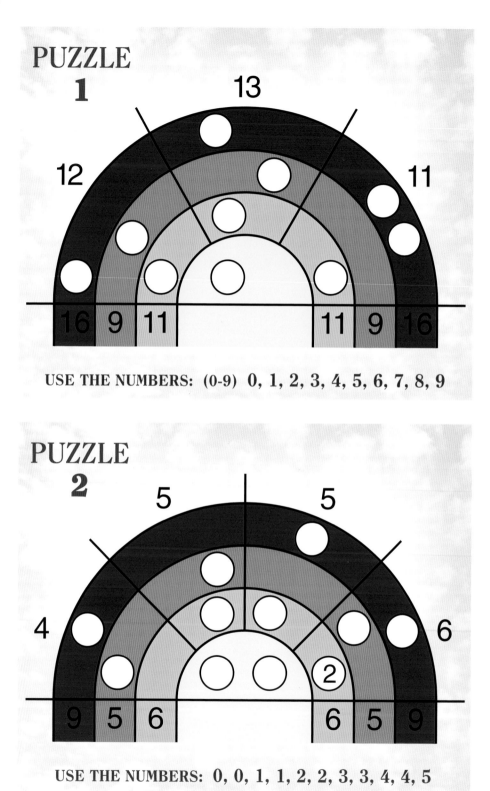

13

12

11

16 9 11 11 9 16

USE THE NUMBERS: (0-9) 0, 1, 2, 3, 4, 5, 6, 7, 8, 9

PUZZLE 2

5   5

4   6

9 5 6 6 5 9

2

USE THE NUMBERS: 0, 0, 1, 1, 2, 2, 3, 3, 4, 4, 5

DIRECTIONS FOR SOLVING ARE ON PAGE 40   ANSWERS ON PAGE 130

PUZZLE
3

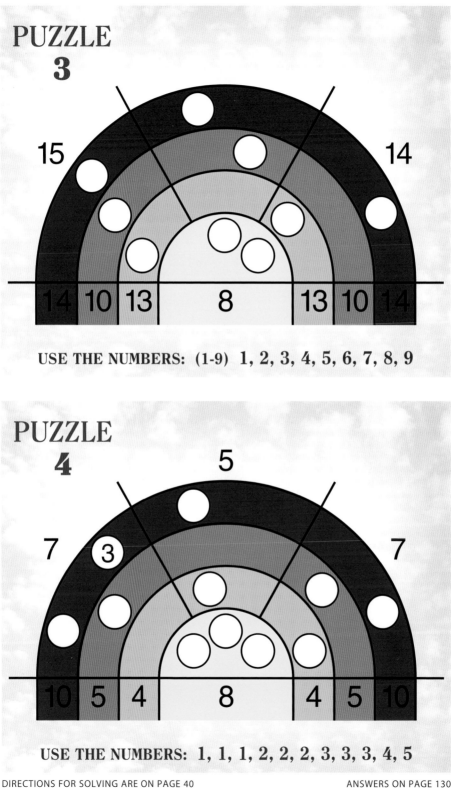

15   14

14 | 10 | 13 | 8 | 13 | 10 | 14

USE THE NUMBERS: (1-9) 1, 2, 3, 4, 5, 6, 7, 8, 9

PUZZLE
4

5

7   ③   7

10 | 5 | 4 | 8 | 4 | 5 | 10

USE THE NUMBERS: 1, 1, 1, 2, 2, 2, 3, 3, 3, 4, 5

DIRECTIONS FOR SOLVING ARE ON PAGE 40   ANSWERS ON PAGE 130

PUZZLE 5

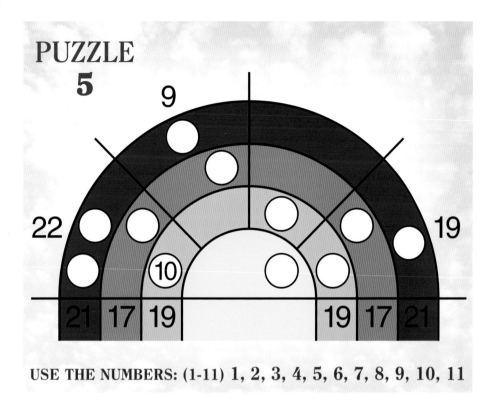

USE THE NUMBERS: (1-11) **1, 2, 3, 4, 5, 6, 7, 8, 9, 10, 11**

PUZZLE 6

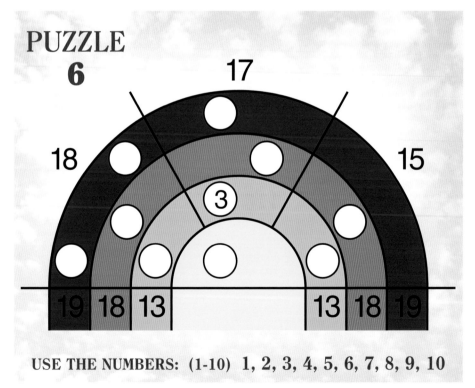

USE THE NUMBERS: (1-10) **1, 2, 3, 4, 5, 6, 7, 8, 9, 10**

DIRECTIONS FOR SOLVING ARE ON PAGE 40   ANSWERS ON PAGE 130

PUZZLE 7

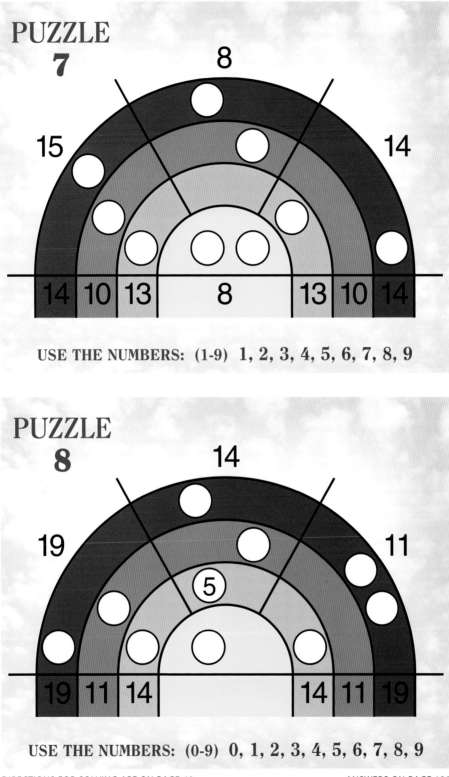

USE THE NUMBERS: (1-9) 1, 2, 3, 4, 5, 6, 7, 8, 9

PUZZLE 8

USE THE NUMBERS: (0-9) 0, 1, 2, 3, 4, 5, 6, 7, 8, 9

DIRECTIONS FOR SOLVING ARE ON PAGE 40

ANSWERS ON PAGE 130

PUZZLE 9

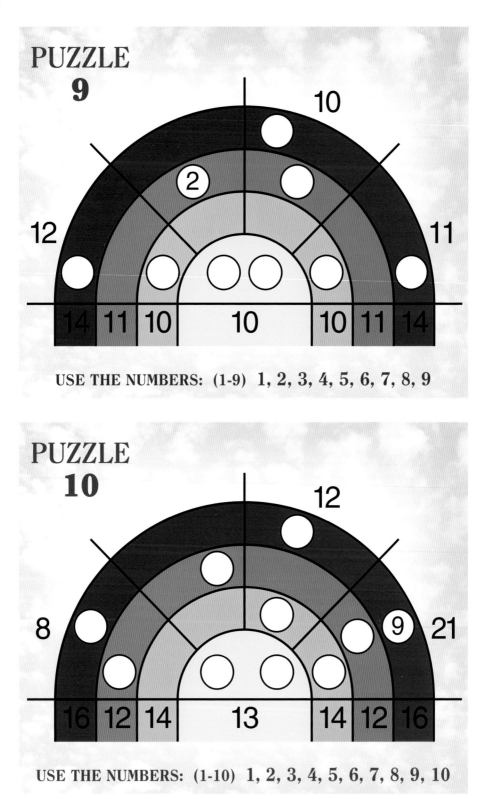

USE THE NUMBERS: (1-9) 1, 2, 3, 4, 5, 6, 7, 8, 9

PUZZLE 10

USE THE NUMBERS: (1-10) 1, 2, 3, 4, 5, 6, 7, 8, 9, 10

DIRECTIONS FOR SOLVING ARE ON PAGE 40   ANSWERS ON PAGE 130

PUZZLE
11

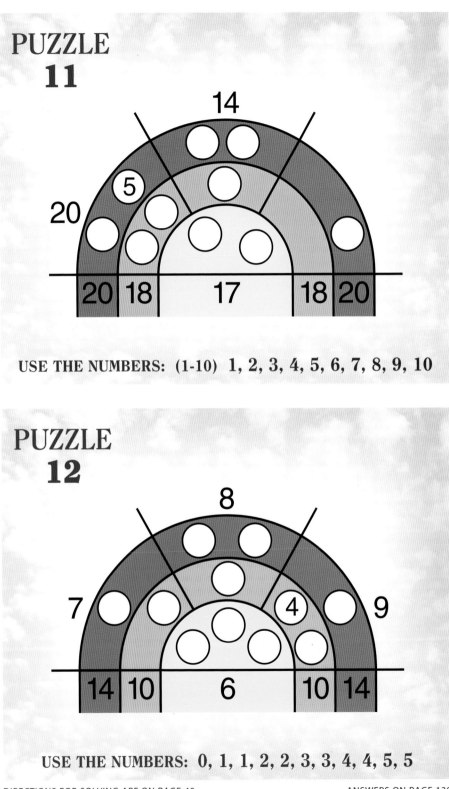

14

5

20

20 | 18 | 17 | 18 | 20

USE THE NUMBERS: (1-10) 1, 2, 3, 4, 5, 6, 7, 8, 9, 10

PUZZLE
12

8

7

4

9

14 | 10 | 6 | 10 | 14

USE THE NUMBERS: 0, 1, 1, 2, 2, 3, 3, 4, 4, 5, 5

DIRECTIONS FOR SOLVING ARE ON PAGE 40   ANSWERS ON PAGE 130

PUZZLE **1**

2 4 7 9 11		1 3 5 6 8 10	
			■	(24)
				(19)
■				(17)
(20)		(19)	

PUZZLE **2**

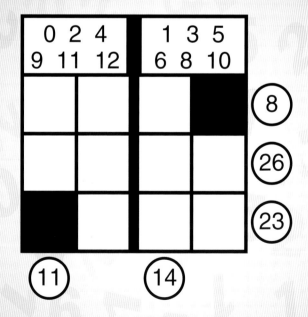

0 2 4 9 11 12		1 3 5 6 8 10	
			■	(8)
				(26)
■				(23)
(11)		(14)	

PUZZLE **3**

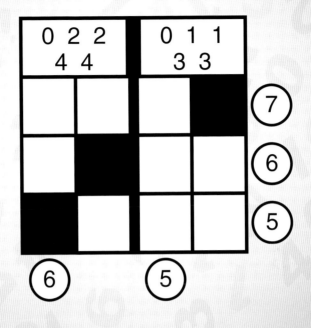

PUZZLE **4**

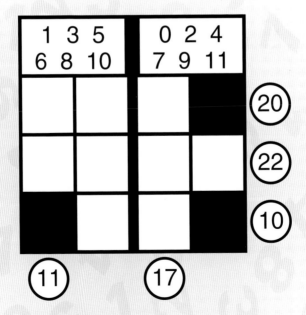

DIRECTIONS FOR SOLVING ARE ON PAGE 47

ANSWERS ON PAGE 131

PUZZLE **5**

PUZZLE **6**

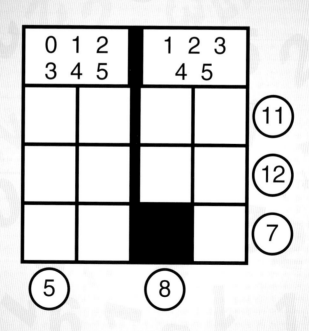

DIRECTIONS FOR SOLVING ARE ON PAGE 47

ANSWERS ON PAGE 131

PUZZLE **7**

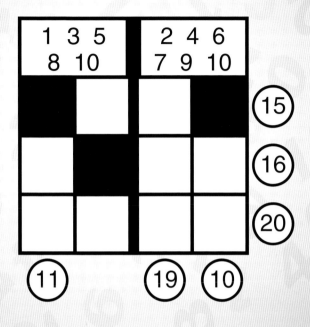

PUZZLE **8**

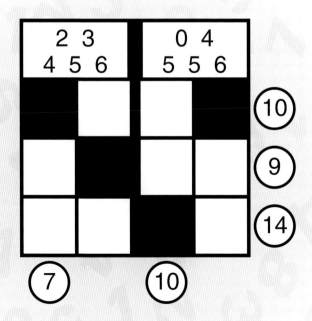

PUZZLE **9**

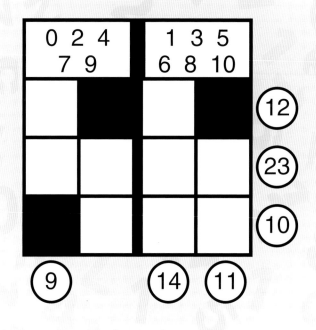

PUZZLE **10**

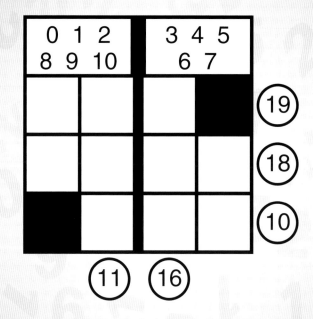

PUZZLE **11**

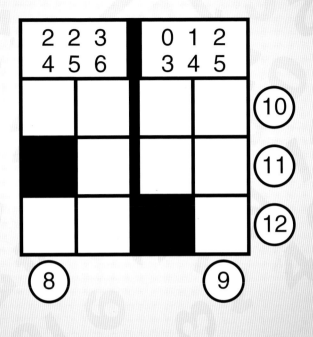

PUZZLE **12**

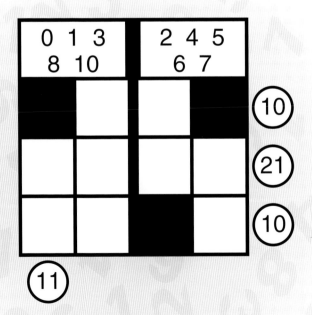

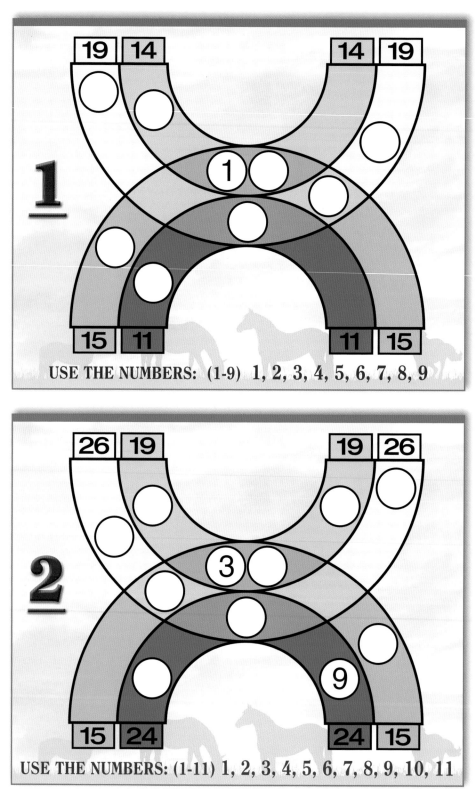

1

| 19 | 14 | | 14 | 19 |

1

| 15 | 11 | | 11 | 15 |

USE THE NUMBERS: (1-9) 1, 2, 3, 4, 5, 6, 7, 8, 9

2

| 26 | 19 | | 19 | 26 |

3

9

| 15 | 24 | | 24 | 15 |

USE THE NUMBERS: (1-11) 1, 2, 3, 4, 5, 6, 7, 8, 9, 10, 11

DIRECTIONS FOR SOLVING ARE ON PAGE 54 ANSWERS ON PAGE 132

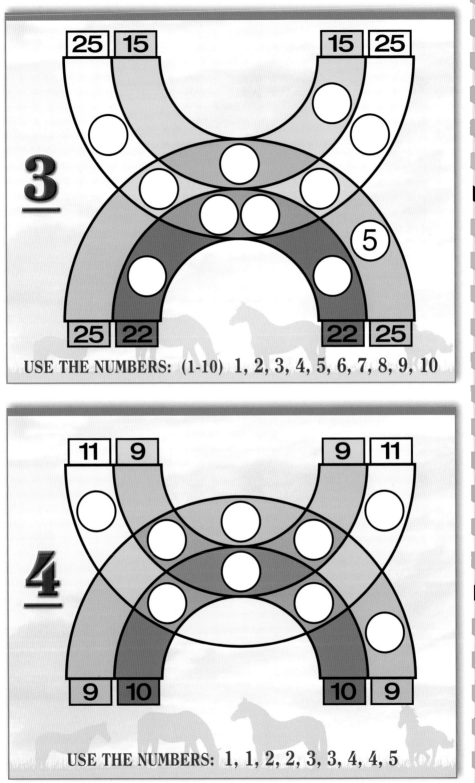

3

25 15   15 25

5

25 22   22 25

USE THE NUMBERS: (1-10) 1, 2, 3, 4, 5, 6, 7, 8, 9, 10

4

11 9   9 11

9 10   10 9

USE THE NUMBERS: 1, 1, 2, 2, 3, 3, 4, 4, 5

DIRECTIONS FOR SOLVING ARE ON PAGE 54   ANSWERS ON PAGE 132

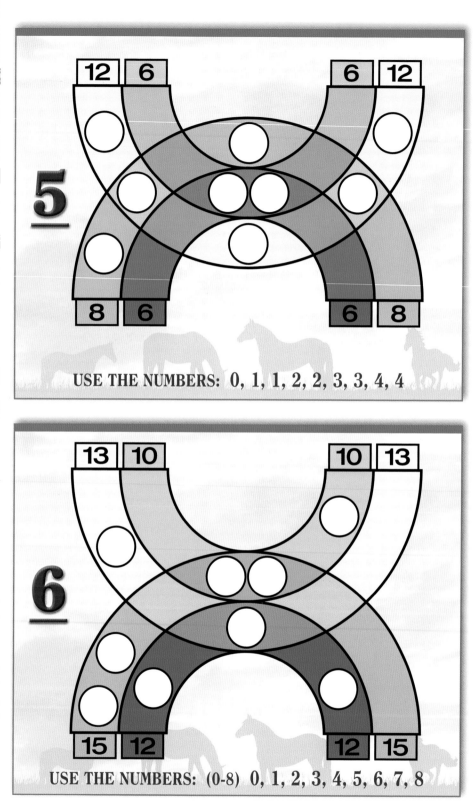

5

| 12 | 6 | | 6 | 12 |

| 8 | 6 | | 6 | 8 |

USE THE NUMBERS: 0, 1, 1, 2, 2, 3, 3, 4, 4

6

| 13 | 10 | | 10 | 13 |

| 15 | 12 | | 12 | 15 |

USE THE NUMBERS: (0-8) 0, 1, 2, 3, 4, 5, 6, 7, 8

DIRECTIONS FOR SOLVING ARE ON PAGE 54

ANSWERS ON PAGE 132

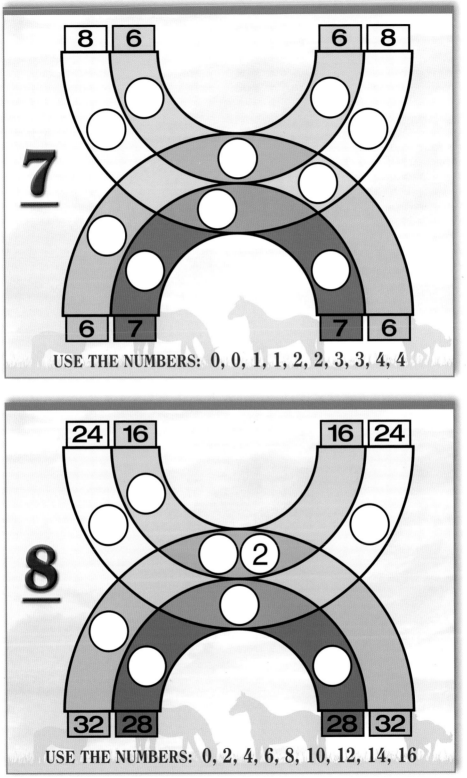

7

USE THE NUMBERS: 0, 0, 1, 1, 2, 2, 3, 3, 4, 4

8

USE THE NUMBERS: 0, 2, 4, 6, 8, 10, 12, 14, 16

DIRECTIONS FOR SOLVING ARE ON PAGE 54

ANSWERS ON PAGE 132

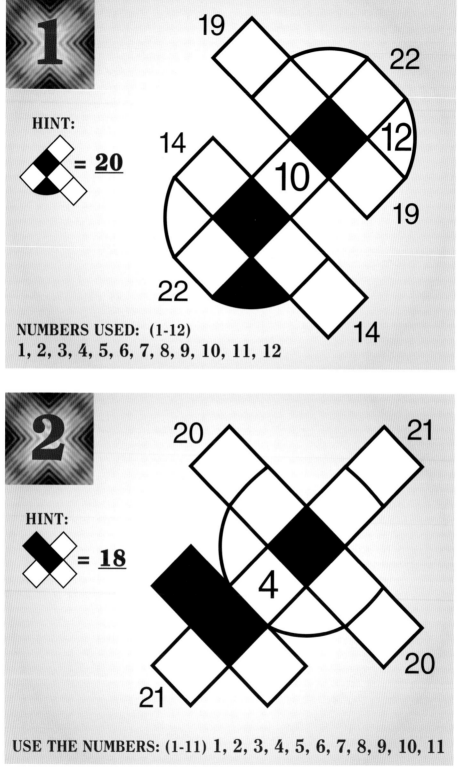

1

HINT:

= **20**

19 22 12 10 19 14 22 14

NUMBERS USED: (1-12)
1, 2, 3, 4, 5, 6, 7, 8, 9, 10, 11, 12

2

HINT:

= **18**

20 21 4 21 20

USE THE NUMBERS: (1-11) 1, 2, 3, 4, 5, 6, 7, 8, 9, 10, 11

DIRECTIONS FOR SOLVING ARE ON PAGE 59   ANSWERS ON PAGE 133

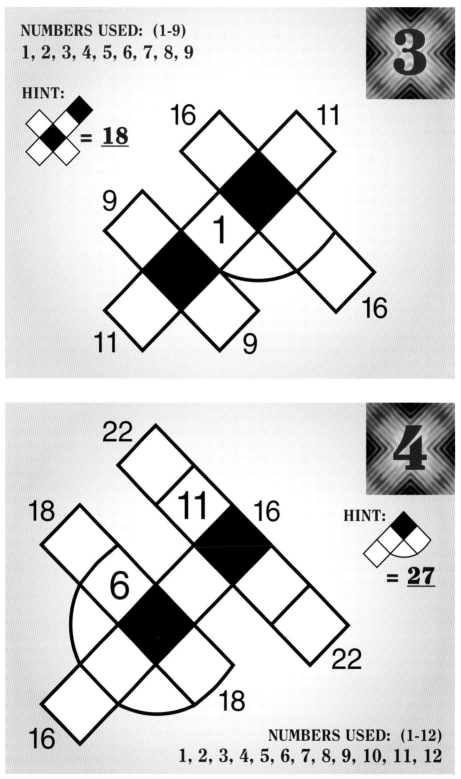

NUMBERS USED: (1-9)
1, 2, 3, 4, 5, 6, 7, 8, 9

3

HINT: = **18**

16   11

9

1

11   9

16

22

4

18   11   16

HINT: = **27**

6

22

16   18

NUMBERS USED: (1-12)
1, 2, 3, 4, 5, 6, 7, 8, 9, 10, 11, 12

DIRECTIONS FOR SOLVING ARE ON PAGE 59   ANSWERS ON PAGE 133

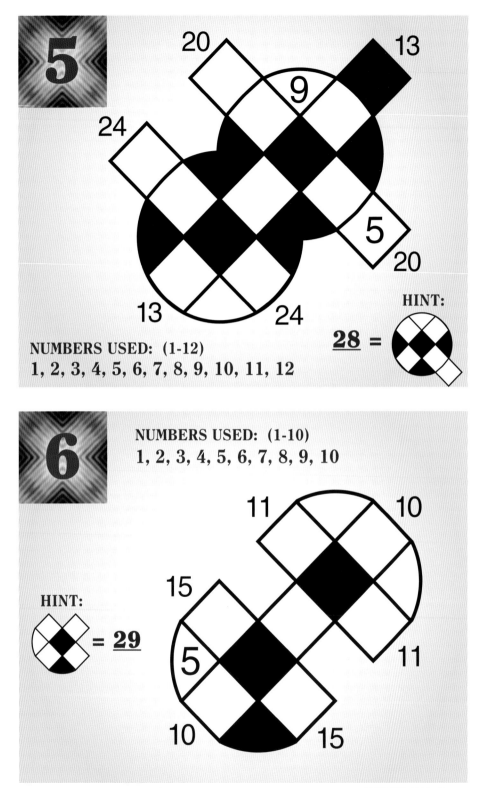

5

20 13

9

24

5

20

13 24

HINT:

28 =

NUMBERS USED: (1-12)
1, 2, 3, 4, 5, 6, 7, 8, 9, 10, 11, 12

6

NUMBERS USED: (1-10)
1, 2, 3, 4, 5, 6, 7, 8, 9, 10

11 10

15

HINT:

= **29**

5

11

10 15

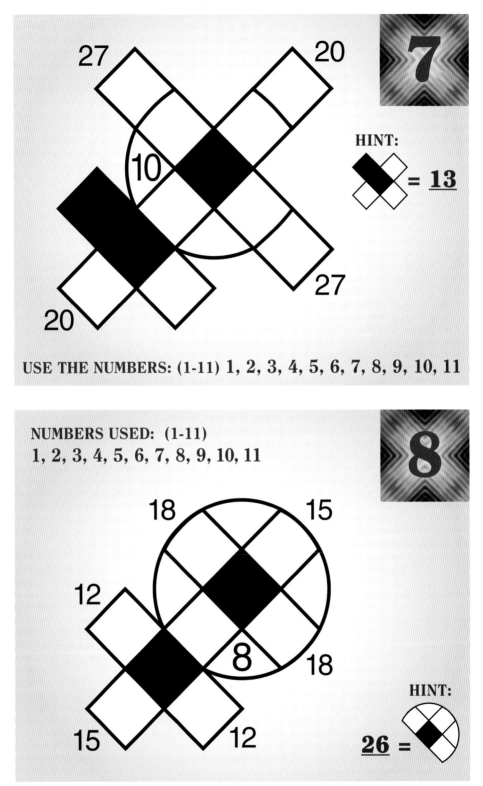

7

HINT:

= **13**

USE THE NUMBERS: (1-11) 1, 2, 3, 4, 5, 6, 7, 8, 9, 10, 11

8

NUMBERS USED: (1-11)
1, 2, 3, 4, 5, 6, 7, 8, 9, 10, 11

HINT:

26 =

DIRECTIONS FOR SOLVING ARE ON PAGE 59   ANSWERS ON PAGE 133

9

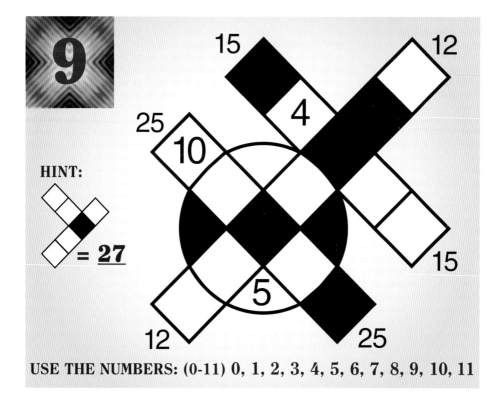

HINT:

= **27**

USE THE NUMBERS: (0-11) 0, 1, 2, 3, 4, 5, 6, 7, 8, 9, 10, 11

10

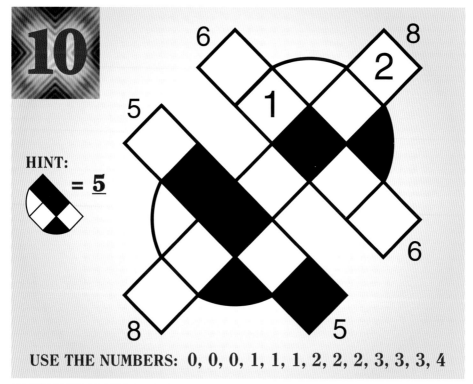

HINT:

= **5**

USE THE NUMBERS: 0, 0, 0, 1, 1, 1, 2, 2, 2, 3, 3, 3, 4

DIRECTIONS FOR SOLVING ARE ON PAGE 59 ANSWERS ON PAGE 133

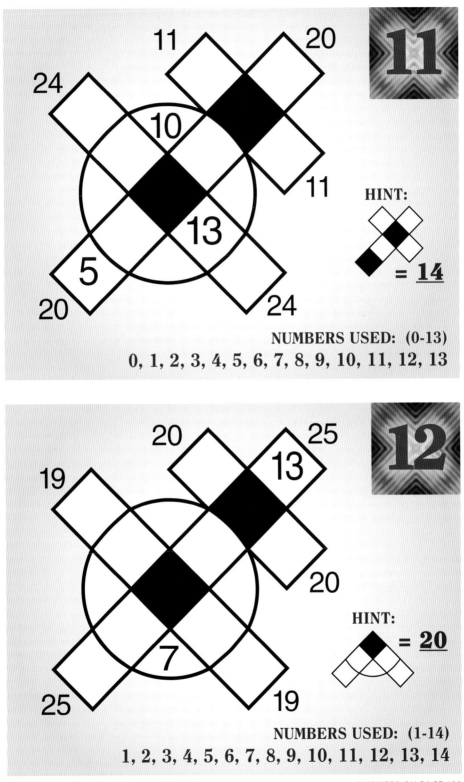

11

24 11 20

10

11

13

5

20 24

HINT:

= **14**

NUMBERS USED: (0-13)
0, 1, 2, 3, 4, 5, 6, 7, 8, 9, 10, 11, 12, 13

12

20 25

19 13

20

25 7 19

HINT:

= **20**

NUMBERS USED: (1-14)
1, 2, 3, 4, 5, 6, 7, 8, 9, 10, 11, 12, 13, 14

DIRECTIONS FOR SOLVING ARE ON PAGE 59

ANSWERS ON PAGE 133

"SAME SUM" PUZZLE ANSWERS

Almost all puzzles have more than one solution.

PUZZLE 1

SUMS OF 16

PUZZLE 2
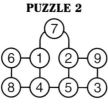
SUMS OF 19

PUZZLE 3
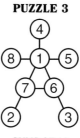
SUMS OF 14

PUZZLE 4
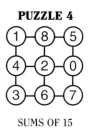
SUMS OF 15

PUZZLE 5
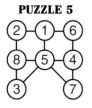
SUMS OF 16

PUZZLE 6

SUMS OF 18

PUZZLE 7
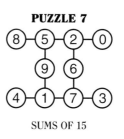
SUMS OF 15

PUZZLE 8
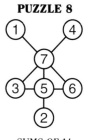
SUMS OF 14

PUZZLE 9
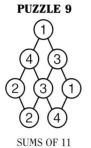
SUMS OF 11

PUZZLE 10

SUMS OF 17

PUZZLE 11

SUMS OF 10

PUZZLE 12
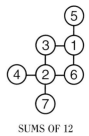
SUMS OF 12

PUZZLE 13
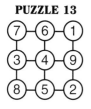
SUMS OF 20

PUZZLE 14
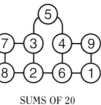
SUMS OF 20

PUZZLE 15
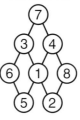
SUMS OF 15

PUZZLE 16

SUMS OF 15

"SAME SUM" PUZZLE ANSWERS

Almost all puzzles have more than one solution.

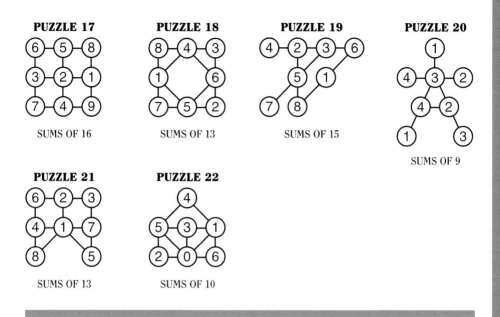

PUZZLE 17

SUMS OF 16

PUZZLE 18

SUMS OF 13

PUZZLE 19

SUMS OF 15

PUZZLE 20

SUMS OF 9

PUZZLE 21

SUMS OF 13

PUZZLE 22

SUMS OF 10

"HONEYCOMB" PUZZLE ANSWERS

Almost all puzzles have more than one solution.

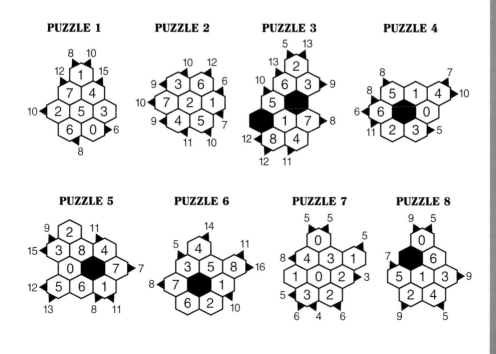

PUZZLE 1

PUZZLE 2

PUZZLE 3

PUZZLE 4

PUZZLE 5

PUZZLE 6

PUZZLE 7

PUZZLE 8

"HONEYCOMB" PUZZLE ANSWERS

Almost all puzzles have more than one solution.

PUZZLE 9

PUZZLE 10
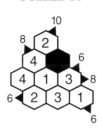

PUZZLE 11
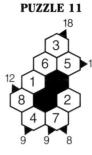

PUZZLE 12
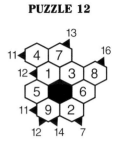

PUZZLE 13
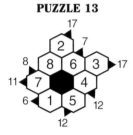

PUZZLE 14
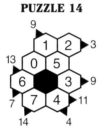

PUZZLE 15
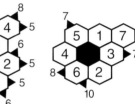

PUZZLE 16
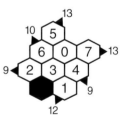

PUZZLE 17
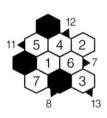

PUZZLE 18

PUZZLE 19
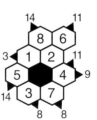

PUZZLE 20

PUZZLE 21
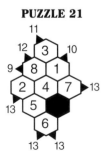

PUZZLE 22
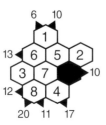

PUZZLE 23
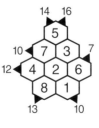

PUZZLE 24
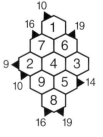

"CHOPSTICK" PUZZLE ANSWERS

Almost all puzzles have more than one solution.

PUZZLE 1

PUZZLE 2

PUZZLE 3

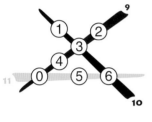

PUZZLE 4

PUZZLE 5

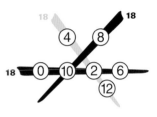

PUZZLE 6

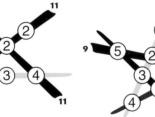

PUZZLE 7

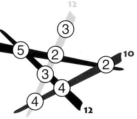

PUZZLE 8

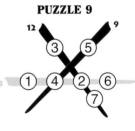

PUZZLE 9

PUZZLE 10

PUZZLE 11

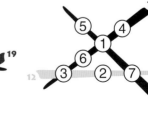

PUZZLE 12

121

"RISING SUN" PUZZLE ANSWERS

Almost all puzzles have more than one solution.

PUZZLE 1
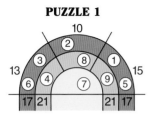

PUZZLE 2
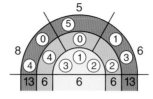

PUZZLE 3
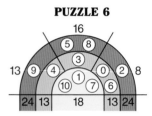

PUZZLE 4
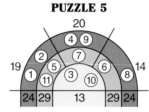

PUZZLE 5

PUZZLE 6
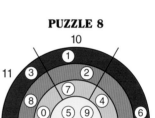

PUZZLE 7
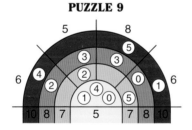

PUZZLE 8
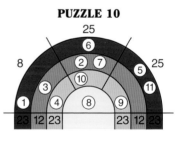

PUZZLE 9
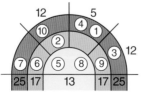

PUZZLE 10
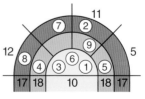

PUZZLE 11

PUZZLE 12

"NUMBER SELECT" PUZZLE ANSWERS

Almost all puzzles have more than one solution.

PUZZLE 1

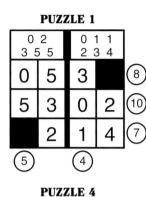

0 2 3 5 5		0 1 1 2 3 4		
0	5	3	■	(8)
5	3	0	2	(10)
■	2	1	4	(7)
(5)		(4)		

PUZZLE 2

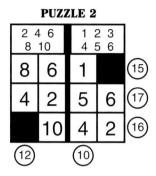

2 4 6 8 10		1 2 3 4 5 6		
8	6	1	■	(15)
4	2	5	6	(17)
■	10	4	2	(16)
(12)		(10)		

PUZZLE 3

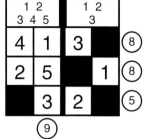

1 2 3 4 5		1 2 3		
4	1	3	■	(8)
2	5	■	1	(8)
■	3	2	■	(5)
(9)				

PUZZLE 4

1 2 3 4		0 1 2		
■	4	1	■	(5)
1	■	■	2	(3)
3	2	■	0	(5)
(4)				

PUZZLE 5

1 3 5 8 10 12		2 4 6 7 9 11		
1	3	2	6	(12)
5	10	9	11	(35)
12	8	■	4	(24)
(18)		(11)		

PUZZLE 6

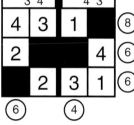

2 2 3 4		1 1 4 3		
4	3	1	■	(8)
2	■	■	4	(6)
■	2	3	1	(6)
(6)		(4)		

PUZZLE 7

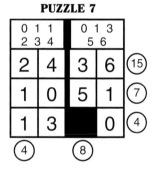

0 1 1 2 3 4		0 1 3 5 6		
2	4	3	6	(15)
1	0	5	1	(7)
1	3	■	0	(4)
(4)		(8)		

PUZZLE 8

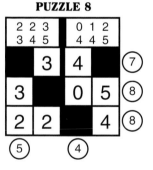

2 2 3 3 4 5		0 1 2 4 4 5		
■	3	4	■	(7)
3	■	0	5	(8)
2	2	■	4	(8)
(5)		(4)		

PUZZLE 9

1 2 3 5		2 4 6		
1	■	6	■	
2	3	■	2	(7)
5	■	4		(9)
(8)		(10)		

PUZZLE 10

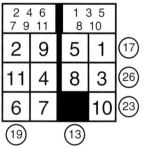

2 4 6 7 9 11		1 3 5 8 10		
2	9	5	1	(17)
11	4	8	3	(26)
6	7	■	10	(23)
(19)		(13)		

PUZZLE 11

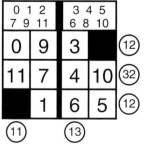

0 1 2 7 9 11		3 4 5 6 8 10		
0	9	3	■	(12)
11	7	4	10	(32)
■	1	6	5	(12)
(11)		(13)		

PUZZLE 12

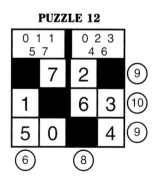

0 1 1 5 7		0 2 3 4 6		
■	7	2	■	(9)
1	■	6	3	(10)
5	0	■	4	(9)
(6)		(8)		

"HORSESHOE" PUZZLE ANSWERS

Almost all puzzles have more than one solution.

PUZZLE 1
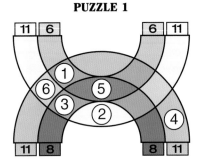

PUZZLE 2
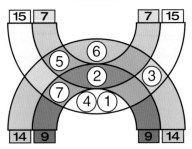

PUZZLE 3
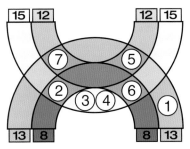

PUZZLE 4
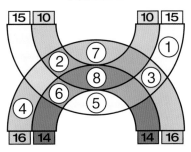

PUZZLE 5
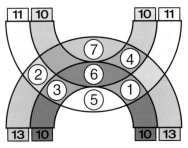

PUZZLE 6
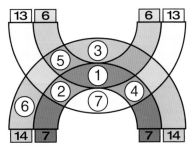

PUZZLE 7
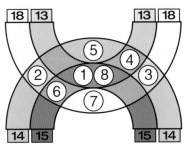

PUZZLE 8
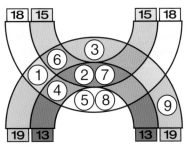

"X" FACTOR PUZZLE ANSWERS

Almost all puzzles have more than one solution.

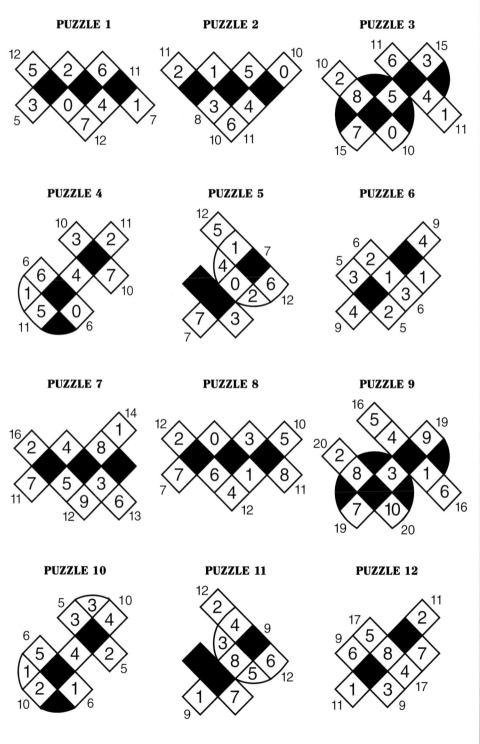

MORE CHALLENGING "SAME SUM" PUZZLE ANSWERS

Almost all puzzles have more than one solution.

PUZZLE 1

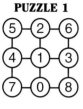

SUMS OF 12

PUZZLE 2

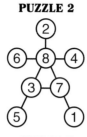

SUMS OF 18

PUZZLE 3

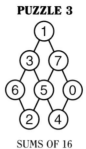

SUMS OF 16

PUZZLE 4

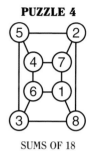

SUMS OF 18

PUZZLE 5

SUMS OF 14

PUZZLE 6

SUMS OF 18

PUZZLE 7

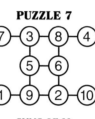

SUMS OF 22

PUZZLE 8

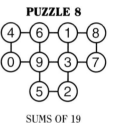

SUMS OF 19

PUZZLE 9

SUMS OF 16

PUZZLE 10

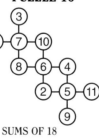

SUMS OF 18

PUZZLE 11

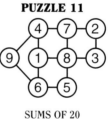

SUMS OF 20

PUZZLE 12

SUMS OF 15

PUZZLE 13

SUMS OF 18

PUZZLE 14

SUMS OF 10

PUZZLE 15

SUMS OF 16

PUZZLE 16

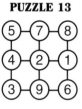

SUMS OF 12

MORE CHALLENGING "SAME SUM" PUZZLE ANSWERS

Almost all puzzles have more than one solution.

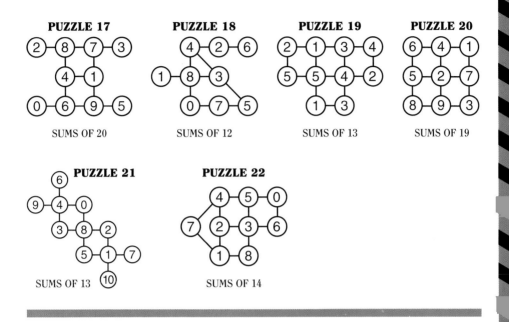

PUZZLE 17

SUMS OF 20

PUZZLE 18

SUMS OF 12

PUZZLE 19

SUMS OF 13

PUZZLE 20

SUMS OF 19

PUZZLE 21

SUMS OF 13

PUZZLE 22

SUMS OF 14

MORE CHALLENGING "HONEYCOMB" PUZZLE ANSWERS

Almost all puzzles have more than one solution.

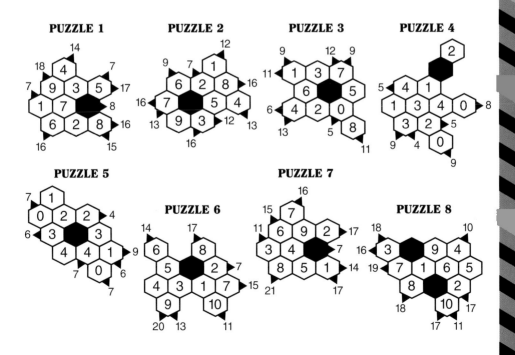

PUZZLE 1

PUZZLE 2

PUZZLE 3

PUZZLE 4

PUZZLE 5

PUZZLE 6

PUZZLE 7

PUZZLE 8

MORE CHALLENGING "HONEYCOMB" PUZZLE ANSWERS

Almost all puzzles have more than one solution.

PUZZLE 9

7
2   5
6 4 3 3 10
10 5 1 4 19
2 1 0 5 8
11   7   12

PUZZLE 10

16 19
17 3 1 9 13
4 11 5 20
2 7 10
9 6 8
20   22

PUZZLE 11

19 4 12
2 5 9 16
10 7 3
10 8 1 19
11 6 13
23

PUZZLE 12

7   5   8
6 0 2 1 3
3 4
4 1 5
0 2
5   5

PUZZLE 13

17   10   12
12 5 1 2 4
9 8
3 0
7 6
12   7

PUZZLE 14

4
9 1 3
3 3 2 8
4 4 0
1 4
9 2

PUZZLE 15

12
15 5 11
2 7 6 15
0 4
3 8
10 1

PUZZLE 16

10   12
8 1
2 6
7 9 4 20
5 3
12   18
9

PUZZLE 17

9
1   7
1 4 6
2 3 2 7
7 3 0 4 0
6   6

PUZZLE 18

17 7
2 3 10 15
9 4 13
12 6 1 8 15
5 5 22
16

PUZZLE 19

5
7 3 4
18 9 8 0 1
12 6 2 8 5
23 15 7
20

PUZZLE 20

7   5
5 4 0 1
2 4
6 2 1 3
4   7 3
6

PUZZLE 21

15
8 11
11 5 6
3 7 10
10 2 4 1 17
9
23
17 21

PUZZLE 22

12
12 8 18
3 6
1 5 7 13
9
4 2
21

PUZZLE 23

25
8 17
13 5 11 7 23
14 9 2 3
1 4 10 6 21
15 20 20

PUZZLE 24

9   10
5
3 3
8 4 4
2 1 5 1 9
2
8
7 14

MORE CHALLENGING "CHOPSTICK" PUZZLE ANSWERS

Almost all puzzles have more than one solution.

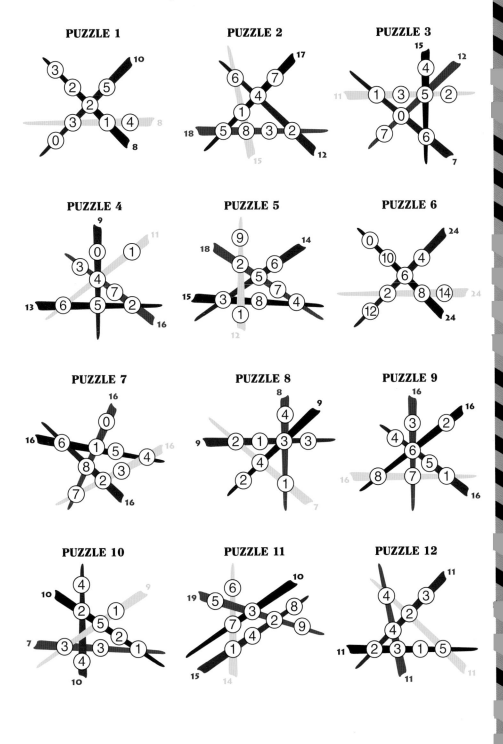

MORE CHALLENGING "RISING SUN" PUZZLE ANSWERS

Almost all puzzles have more than one solution.

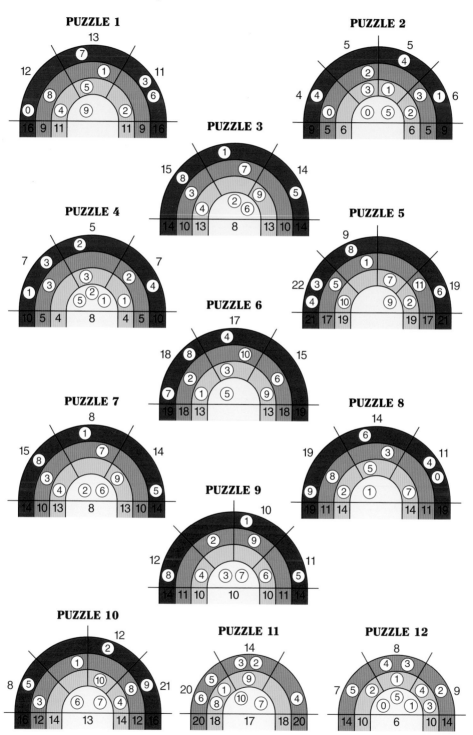

MORE CHALLENGING "NUMBER SELECT" PUZZLE ANSWERS

Almost all puzzles have more than one solution.

MORE CHALLENGING "HORSESHOE" PUZZLE ANSWERS

Almost all puzzles have more than one solution.

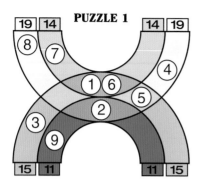

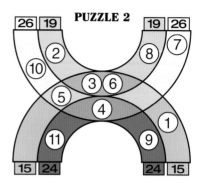

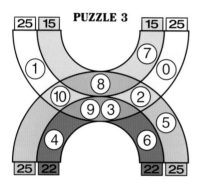

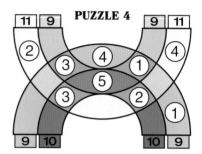

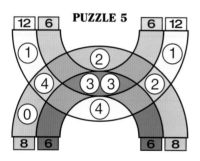

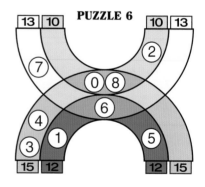

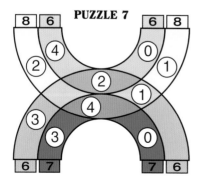

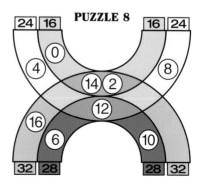

MORE CHALLENGING "X" FACTOR PUZZLE ANSWERS

Almost all puzzles have more than one solution.

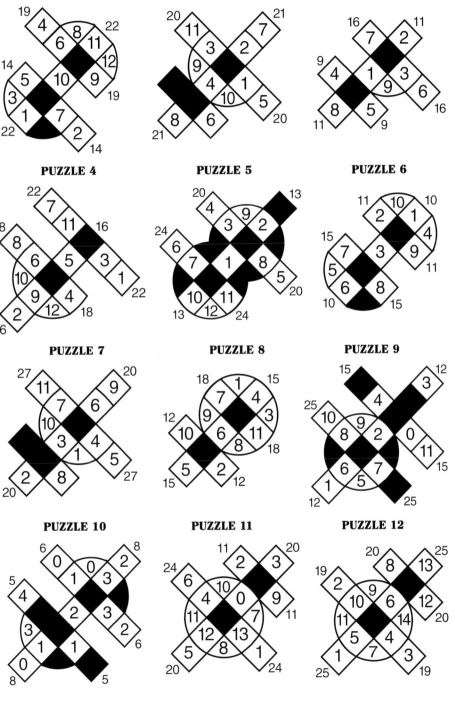

NOTES

NOTES